ELEMENTARY
ACCOUNTING

*the text of this book is printed
on 100% recycled paper*

About the Authors

Royal D. M. Bauer received a Master of Business Administration degree from Northwestern University. From 1941 to 1969 he was professor of accounting at the University of Missouri. He is a certified public accountant and a member of many professional organizations. In addition to *Elementary Accounting* he has had numerous articles published and is coauthor of *Auditing*.

Paul Holland Darby received a Master of Arts degree from the University of Missouri. He has taught at Christian College, Kemper Military School and College, and Central Methodist College, all of which are located in Missouri. A certified public accountant, Mr. Darby has had extensive experience in his field.

ELEMENTARY ACCOUNTING

FOURTH EDITION

Royal D. M. Bauer, C.P.A.
Paul Holland Darby, C.P.A.

BARNES & NOBLE BOOKS

A DIVISION OF HARPER & ROW, PUBLISHERS

New York, Hagerstown, San Francisco, London

ELEMENTARY ACCOUNTING, FOURTH EDITION. Copyright 1942, 1945, 1952 by Barnes & Noble, Inc. Copyright © 1973 by Royal D. M. Bauer. All rights reserved. Printed in the United States of America. No part of this book may be used or reproduced in any manner without written permission except in the case of brief quotations embodied in critical articles and reviews. For information address Harper & Row, Publishers, Inc., 10 East 53d Street, New York, N.Y. 10022. Published simultaneously in Canada by Fitzhenry & Whiteside Limited, Toronto.

First BARNES & NOBLE BOOKS edition published 1973.

LIBRARY OF CONGRESS CATALOG CARD NUMBER: 72–7763

ISBN: 0-06-460150-1

79 80 81 82   10 9 8 7

Contents

Preface

This book attempts to outline for the reader the principles underlying modern accounting procedures in a brief, yet reasonably comprehensive, manner.

It is intended to meet the needs of several groups of persons, as follows:

1. Business and professional persons who need more information about accounting fundamentals

2. Accountants and bookkeepers who wish to have a concise elementary book available for occasional reference

3. Students who want a preliminary survey of specific materials, a constant aid to study, and a review of the elements of accounting previously studied

4. All others who desire to increase their understanding of the methods employed to record business transactions.

The reader should bear in mind that variations are possible and even desirable in many accounting procedures, and that an adequate presentation of the subject cannot be confined to one simplified method of approach. Therefore, alternative methods and synonymous terms are included in this book where necessary.

How to Study Accounting

In the study of accounting, it is desirable to follow accepted procedures in order to avoid wasted effort. The following suggestions may help the student obtain the best results for the time devoted to his studies.[1]

Reading. Speed of reading, though desirable in many situations, is not stressed in the study of accounting, which requires reading for detailed information. It is well, however, to skim rapidly through a chapter for a quick overview before reading slowly for comprehension.

When reading an accounting text, the reader should study each example given. Answers should be found to such questions as: What was done? What was the sequence? Where did this information come from? Where did it go?

Using the Library. Most libraries have a wealth of material available, including reference books and a number of standard texts, for supplementary use with any accounting textbook. This material is usually found in the 657 section of libraries using the Dewey decimal system. Reference books may be used for further review or for intensive study of particular phases of accounting. Standard texts provide an opportunity for parallel study, so that the reader can see how different authors treat the same subject. Both reference books and textbooks are helpful when judiciously used.

Outlining and Note Taking. By putting the authors' ideas or the teacher's lectures into his own words, the student will clarify his own thoughts and gain an aid for review.

1. For a more comprehensive discussion of this subject, see *Best Methods of Study* by Samuel Smith et al., published by Barnes & Noble Books, a division of Harper & Row (New York, 1970).

Reviewing. Reviewing consists of a brief survey of the material studied. It may include the scanning of books already read, self-testing, study of notes, and the use of this book as an outline. A review is an aid to comprehension, especially if it is made accurately, carefully, and with discrimination.

Studying for periodic and final tests helps the student determine the extent of his own proficiency and discover which topics require further study.

ELEMENTARY
ACCOUNTING

CHAPTER 1

Meaning and Purpose of Accounting

NATURE OF ACCOUNTING

Business records, written on clay tablets in ancient Babylon, have survived over four thousand years. These tablets, containing reports of business transactions inscribed in cuneiform, are the earliest known commercial records.

Today, business transactions are recorded by the method of bookkeeping known as double-entry. Books kept according to this method for the city of Genoa in 1340 are still in existence. The oldest significant treatise on double-entry bookkeeping now known to exist was published in Venice in 1494 by Luca Pacioli, a Franciscan monk, as part of his *Summa de Arithmetica*.

There was little development in the subject of accounting from Pacioli's time until late in the nineteenth century. The growth of industry and commerce following the Industrial Revolution gave impetus to the development of accounting techniques. Large-scale production and the complexity of the modern economic structure have necessitated greatly improved accounting methods and systems. Accounting in its most advanced form, however, is still based on the fundamental concepts developed as early as the fifteenth century.

Accounting may be defined as the mechanism and body of principles by which business activities that are capable of being expressed in terms of money are recorded, classified, and periodically summarized and interpreted.

PURPOSE OF ACCOUNTING

Accounting provides a record of business transactions in financial terms. Accounting records are needed by profit-making enterprises and by nonprofit-making organizations, such as governmental units, fiduciaries, and associations operating for religious, philanthropic, or fraternal purposes. Records of the financial transactions of an individual or a family are considered a necessity at times.

In a business enterprise, managerial decisions, whether of great or small import to the activities of the business, must often rely on the accounting records for information to guide the firm on a profitable and solvent course. Thus, the primary purpose of accounting for any organization is to provide management with the information needed for its efficient operation. Accounting should also make available the financial information properly desired by governmental agencies, present and prospective creditors and investors, and the general public.

BOOKKEEPING DISTINGUISHED FROM ACCOUNTING

Bookkeeping is the systematic recording of business transactions in financial terms. Accounting covers a wider field, which includes bookkeeping and involves the design of business records, data analysis, preparation of reports based on the records, and interpretation of the reports. Usually, the study of bookkeeping emphasizes technique, whereas the study of accounting emphasizes theory.

FINANCIAL STATEMENTS

The three major financial statements are: the *balance sheet*, the *income statement*, and the *statement of changes in financial position* or *funds statement*. The *balance sheet* (statement of financial position) provides a list of assets, liabilities, and proprietorship or capital of a business entity as of a specific date; the *income statement* (statement of operating results) summarizes the income and expenses of a business entity for a specific period of time; and the *funds statement* (statement of changes in financial position) indicates the sources from which funds were acquired during the accounting period covered by the report and the disposition made of them.

BUSINESS TRANSACTIONS

A *business transaction* is an action that involves an exchange of values. It is the occurrence of an event or a condition that is financial in nature and should be recorded in terms of money. Purchases and sales of goods or services are examples. Accounting records show the effects of business transactions on the assets, liabilities, and proprietorship of a business.

COST AND VALUE

Cost, or the price paid for an asset, is the basis ordinarily used in accounting both to record the acquisition and to continue to account for the asset. The amount agreed upon between buyer and seller furnishes an objective measure of the *value* to be recorded; it is a fact established by a completed transaction, not a mere subjective opinion of the value.

Some assets, such as buildings and equipment, gradually depreciate or wear out, and their values on the books are reduced periodically to record the estimated amount of depreciation. As time passes, the amounts reported on the balance sheet based on original or historical cost may no longer approximate current values. Critics of the use of cost under such circumstances have argued that current value should replace cost on the balance sheet. However, in the absence of any generally acceptable objective method for arriving at current values, the traditional use of historical cost continues, although its limitations are becoming more generally recognized.

ACCOUNTING ENTITY

Primarily, accounting records report the results of the transactions of a specific entity. For accounting purposes, the business entity is considered as a separate unit, distinct and apart from any other business or financial interests the owner may have. This concept of the significance of the individual economic unit or business entity is known as the *entity concept*.

Accounting data for a particular unit may be combined, however, with similar data for other units to obtain an overall picture. Such combinations include, for example, the separate divisions of a business enterprise, the units comprising the membership of a national trade association, the constituent parts of a governmental bureau, and other aggregates that can provide useful information.

FORMS OF BUSINESS ORGANIZATION

There are three principal forms of business organization in the United States: *proprietorships, partnerships,* and *corporations.* A *proprietorship* is a business enterprise owned by one person and is formed or discontinued with relative ease. A *partnership* is a business owned by two or more individuals in accordance with a contractual agreement among them. A *corporation* is a legal entity, separate and distinct from its owners, organized under state or national law, in which ownership is divided into shares of capital stock.

UNIVERSAL NEED FOR ACCOUNTING

Benefits from the study of accounting are not restricted to those who specialize in it. Many others find a knowledge of accounting principles useful. In the following three areas of activity, such knowledge is especially valuable.

Bookkeeping and Accounting. One who plans to enter the field of accounting, either as a bookkeeper with routine duties or as an accountant with greater responsibilities, should recognize the need for accounting training.

Business Management. The business executive who has a knowledge of accounting is better enabled to study and interpret financial reports. This ability will help him to evaluate the results of past operations of an enterprise more accurately and to shape its future policies more intelligently.

Personal Record Keeping. Every person, even if he does not plan to be an accountant or a business executive, can benefit from a study of accounting. Such study will enable him to keep better personal records, to understand financial records more readily, and to be more intelligent in his spending, saving, and investing.

SPECIALIZATION IN ACCOUNTING

Accounting activities may be classified, with some degree of overlapping, according to the branches or fields in which accountants specialize, as follows:

1. *General accounting* (including *bookkeeping*), the actual recording process and, possibly, report preparation
2. *Cost accounting*, the determination of business costs, especially unit costs of production and distribution
3. *System building*, the planning, installation, and revision of financial records
4. *Budgetary accounting*, the systematic forecasting of business operations in financial terms
5. *Controllership*, the assumption of responsibility for the accounting records of a firm by its controller, who is the firm's chief accounting officer and one of the financial advisors to its management
6. *Auditing*, the verification of financial records and the preparation of reports thereon, performed (*a*) by independent public accountants or certified public accountants who serve a variety of clients or (*b*) by an internal auditing department consisting of employees of the firm being audited

7. *Tax accounting*, the determination of the correct liability for taxes, especially income taxes and social security taxes, and the preparation of necessary returns
8. *Management services*, a special department set up in many public accounting firms that consults with management on revision of business procedures or initiation of new ones to keep abreast of the best current practices and maintain effective managerial control
9. *Governmental and institutional accounting*, the keeping of financial records and the preparation of reports for governmental units and agencies and nonprofit institutions
10. *Accounting instruction*, the teaching of accounting.

ACCOUNTING AND MODERN BUSINESS

Business Characteristics Leading to Accounting Development. The growth of commerce and industry has brought about the use of more adequate modern accounting records and an increasing interest in such records. Some of the features of present-day business that create a need for modern accounting methods are as follows:

1. *Size.* Business units have grown to unprecedented proportions. *Operations* are too extensive to be comprehended by an individual without summarized reports. *Information for management* must be obtained from accounting reports, since personal inspection of all operations is physically impossible and verbal reports are inadequate. *Objectivity of management* enables policies to be formed without personal bias, but it cannot be maintained in a large business without comprehensive reports.
2. *Complexity of business organizations.* Operation of an enterprise has tended to become more complex under modern economic conditions, necessitating increasing control through accounting.
3. *Separation of management from ownership.* The corporate form of business organization has tended to bring about the existence of managers who are not owners and owners who do not have a direct part in running the business.

Management controls the business, but stockholders control the management, and in order to do this effectively, these owners must have records and reports that clearly indicate what the management has been doing.

4. *Competition.* When competition is keen, profit margins tend to become narrower. Under such conditions, the information to be obtained from accurate accounting records can be especially helpful to management in its endeavor to reduce costs and avoid selling at a price that is economically unsound. At a time when profit margins are narrow, haphazard guessing may be disastrous.

5. *Variety of properties.* Along with the increase in the size of the business unit, there has come a general diversity in the properties owned by a business. This variety of properties may be due to the increase in the number of items produced by one company and also to the large territory that may be served by a single enterprise. *Investment and maintenance policies* relating to property often constitute a major problem in a large concern. *Depreciation policy* presents an involved problem for a business owning a variety of properties, especially if these properties have various lengths of useful life.

6. *Variety of investors.* One of the phenomena of modern business is that the capital required for the operations of an individual enterprise, especially a corporation, may be provided by a large number of persons. Many investors may have varying contractual relationships with the company, and records are necessary to disclose the status of each.

7. *Taxes and government control.* State and federal income tax laws require the exact computation of income. Other laws require periodic reports to various governmental agencies. In order to comply with these laws, there is an additional need for adequate records.

8. *Uniform records.* A former tendency to use accounting methods planned for the convenience of the individual firm has given way to a trend toward greater uniformity in accounting systems.

Statistics are valuable to the businessman in the formation of policies. Comparable accounts are an important source of statistical data.

Business cycles and their accompanying disorders constitute a phenomenon of the modern economic order. Studies of their causes and effects are aided by the information obtainable from uniformly kept accounts. The business cycle increases accounting problems relating to fluctuating prices and the revaluation of assets.

Trade associations in some instances foster the use of uniform records and employ the information obtained from the comparable accounts for the benefit of individual members and the industry as a whole.

Credit studies used to obtain credit from a bank, another concern, or the open market, are simplified when the financial reports on which they are based have been prepared so as to be comparable with similar reports.

Rate making is a difficult problem. Its dependence upon uniform accounting systems is illustrated by the fact that the public utilities are required to use uniform systems established by the rate-making governmental agencies.

RELATIONSHIP OF ACCOUNTING
TO OTHER FIELDS

Viewpoint Contrasted with That of Economics. Economics ordinarily deals with goods and services in society as a whole, whereas accounting is concerned primarily with the individual enterprise. Accounting considers gain or loss of a particular business entity; economics tends to disregard such variations unless they result in a net gain or loss to society.

Accounting and Engineering. Problems arise from time to time that require the combined efforts of engineers and accountants. Examples are: (1) the valuation of buildings and equipment and (2) the distribution of their cost.

Accounting and Law. Taxes, fiduciary relationships, and the formation and dissolution of partnerships and corporations create problems that are best solved by the combined efforts of an accountant and a lawyer. It is desirable that an accountant have some knowledge of the law and a lawyer know something about accounting, but the more complex problems require the competence of experts in each field.

Accounting and Business Management. Accounting is a tool of management. It endeavors to keep such records as will provide the information needed or desired by management.

CHAPTER 2

The Balance Sheet

THE BALANCE SHEET EQUATION

Assets = liabilities + proprietorship. This is the fundamental balance sheet equation. It shows the equality or balance between property, including rights in property, and the claims of owners and others against the property. Its terms may be transposed from one side to the other as in any algebraic equation, for example, *assets − liabilities = proprietorship.* When either the term *liabilities* or the term *equities* is used to include both liabilities and proprietorship, the balance sheet equation becomes *assets = liabilities* or *assets = equities.*

Any form of the balance sheet equation merely shows that assets and the claims against them are equal in value. The claims are of two kinds: those of outside creditors and those of the owner or owners. Creditors' claims are contractual and rank ahead of the residual claims of the owners. In other words, in the event that a business enterprise ceases to operate, its creditors have preferential rights to the assets and must be paid in full before any assets may be distributed to the owners.

ASSETS

Assets may be defined simply as anything of value owned. They consist of rights in property and of property itself, tangible or intangible, applicable to the payments of debts. Among the assets most commonly owned by business enterprises are the following:

1. *Cash,* on hand and in banks, available for current use
2. *Marketable securities* or *temporary investments,* consist-

ing of readily salable securities acquired with temporarily unneeded cash

3. *Notes receivable* or *bills receivable,* written promises of debtors to pay specified amounts, usually with interest, at fixed or determinable future dates

4. *Accounts receivable,* representing amounts collectible, without the formality of notes receivable, from customers or clients for merchandise sold or services rendered on credit

5. *Accrued receivables,* composed of amounts earned, such as interest, rent, royalties, and similar items, but not due to be received until a later date

6. *Merchandise inventory,* goods on hand that are being held for sale

7. *Prepaid expenses,* future expenses paid in advance, such as unexpired insurance, supplies on hand, and prepaid rent expense

8. *Long-term investments,* frequently, securities of other companies that are to be held for a relatively long period of time, generally more than one year

9. *Land,* the ground occupied by business buildings of the enterprise or used for parking lots, outside storage space, and other business operations

10. *Buildings,* structures owned by the enterprise and serving business purposes

11. *Equipment,* including such items as machinery and tools required by manufacturers and service enterprises; furniture and fixtures for factory, workshop, store, and office; and equipment for delivering merchandise that has been sold

12. *Intangible assets,* consisting of the noncurrent and nonmaterial assets of a business, such as patents, trademarks, copyrights, leaseholds, franchises, and goodwill.

LIABILITIES

Liabilities are debts. They consist of obligations to pay money or other assets or to render services to other persons or organizations who are the creditors of the enterprise and who, as a rule, have no voice in its management. The term liabilities is sometimes used in a broad sense to include the claims of both creditors and owners against the assets. The principal types of liabilities are:

1. *Notes payable,* written promises to creditors to repay cash loans or advances of other assets or services
2. *Accounts payable,* representing amounts payable to creditors, without the use of notes payable, for the acquisition of goods or services on a credit basis
3. *Accrued expenses payable,* amounts owed for accumulated business expenses, such as wages, taxes, and interest, but not due to be paid until a later date
4. *Income received in advance,* consisting of income received before it has been earned, such as rent or subscriptions received in advance, for which a liability exists to render agreed-upon services or meet other contractual requirements
5. *Long-term liabilities,* liabilities, such as mortgage notes payable and bonds payable, that will not mature for a comparatively long period of time, usually more than one year.

PROPRIETORSHIP

Proprietorship is the excess of assets over liabilities. It is the owner's equity. It is given such titles as proprietorship, ownership, capital, net worth, proprietor's equity, and stockholders' equity. It represents the ownership of one or more persons who have more or less permanently invested in an enterprise and are primarily responsible for its success.

Equities are all claims against, or rights to, assets. The term thus includes liabilities to creditors and the proprietorship claims of owners. Balance sheet presentation of the claims of owners should indicate the form of business organization. When an individual is the sole proprietor of a business, his equity is frequently expressed on the balance sheet in one amount, but two subdivisions are sometimes shown, such as:

1. *Owner's capital,* representing amounts contributed by the owner as permanent capital
2. *Owner's personal,* or *drawing,* or *current, account,* representing operating profit or loss and the proprietor's with-

drawals for personal use. (Customarily, a personal account is a temporary account and is transferred to a capital account at the end of the year.)

A partnership balance sheet should disclose similar information, but it should be recorded separately for each partner. A corporation balance sheet usually presents the stockholders' equity in at least two parts:

1. *Capital stock,* amounts contributed by stockholders as permanent capital
2. *Retained earnings,* total cumulative earnings less amounts distributed to stockholders as dividends. (Retained earnings, as a caption on corporation balance sheets, has largely replaced the terms *surplus* and *earned surplus,* once generally employed.)

THE STATEMENT

A *balance sheet* is a statement of the financial condition of an individual or enterprise at a given date. The statement is also known by other titles, such as financial statement, statement of financial condition, statement of financial position, statement of assets and liabilities, statement of resources and liabilities, statement of worth, general balance sheet, position statement, and statement of assets, liabilities, and capital.

The balance sheet enumerates the amounts and the nature of the assets, liabilities, and proprietorship, and is an elaboration of the equation, assets = liabilities + proprietorship. At times, it is considered the most important financial statement, the goal of accounting activity. However, the income statement is often of equal, or even greater, importance.

Form of the Balance Sheet. A statement of financial condition does not necessarily follow an orthodox form; but there are two standard forms that have found general acceptance, the *account form* or *horizontal form,* and the *report form* or *vertical form.*

1. *Account form.* This form has the assets placed on the left side of the page and the liabilities and proprietorship on the right side in parallel vertical columns with equal totals. The account form is developed from the equation, assets = liabilities + proprietorship, and derives its name from its similarity to the account, a basic accounting device

described in Chapter 4. An example of the account form of a balance sheet appears in Appendix A, on pages 218 and 219.

2. *Report form.* This form lists the assets and below them the liabilities followed by the proprietorship. One variation of the report form deducts liabilities from assets, the difference being proprietorship. Another variation, which is the one generally used, adds liabilities and proprietorship, their sum being the same as the total assets. The first variation emphasizes the amount of proprietorship and is based on the equation, assets − liabilities = proprietorship. The second variation emphasizes the equality of assets and equities, as does the account form, and both are based on the equation, assets = liabilities + proprietorship. Following are two illustrative balance sheets prepared in the report form. The first deducts liabilities from assets to arrive at the proprietorship total; the second shows that the sum of liabilities and proprietorship is equal to the total assets.

McINERNY REAL ESTATE COMPANY

BALANCE SHEET
DECEMBER 31, 19- -

Assets		
Cash		$ 5,440
Rental commissions receivable		280
Office supplies		400
Automobile	$ 5,600	
Less accumulated depreciation	2,100	3,500
Office equipment	$ 4,400	
Less accumulated depreciation	1,110	3,290
Total assets		$12,910
Deduct liabilities		
Commissions payable	$ 300	
Taxes payable	1,040	1,340
Excess of assets over liabilities—proprietorship		$11,570
Proprietorship		
William J. McInerny, capital, January 1, 19- -		$10,450
Net income for the year 19- -	$21,120	
Less withdrawals	20,000	1,120
Capital, December 31, 19- -		$11,570

COOK MERCANTILE COMPANY

BALANCE SHEET
JANUARY 31, 19--

ASSETS

Current assets
Cash		$ 4,750
Marketable securities		3,000
Accounts receivable, customers	$16,250	
Less estimated uncollectible accounts	300	15,950
Accrued interest receivable		90
Merchandise inventory		32,430
Supplies on hand		320
Prepaid insurance		640
Total current assets		$ 57,180

Fixed assets
Land		$ 12,000
Building	$60,000	
Less accumulated depreciation	6,000	54,000
Store equipment	$11,000	
Less accumulated depreciation	3,300	7,700
Office equipment	$ 3,000	
Less accumulated depreciation	900	2,100
Total fixed assets		75,800
Total assets		$132,980

EQUITIES

Current liabilities
Accounts payable, trade creditors		$12,940
Accrued wages payable		310
Taxes payable		1,600
Rent received in advance		200
Total liabilities		$ 15,050

Owner's equity
Henry Cook, capital, February 1, 19--		$116,000
Net income, year ended January 31, 19--	$15,430	
Less withdrawals	13,500	
Increase in capital		1,930
Henry Cook, capital, January 31, 19--		117,930
Total equities		$132,980

CLASSIFICATION OF ASSETS AND LIABILITIES

Assets and liabilities generally appear on the balance sheet in classified groups in order to make them more readily understandable. Two orders of presentation are common, one placing the current groups before the fixed groups and the other placing the fixed groups before the current groups. The latter arrangement was widely used at one time, but the present tendency is to place the current groups first.

Current Assets consist of cash available for current use and other assets that will normally be sold or converted into cash or consumed within one year or one normal operating cycle, whichever is longer. An *operating cycle* is the average length of time between the purchase of merchandise and the reconversion of this merchandise to cash. Current assets are known by a variety of terms having approximately the same meaning, such as *current, liquid, quick, active, turnover, working, circulating,* and *floating* assets. They are composed of items that are constantly changing and vary in volume with the changing volume of business. This concept of current assets includes prepaid expenses.

Prepaid Expenses consist of goods or services that have been acquired for use in the business, and in the near future, in the ordinary course of operations, will be consumed. This group of assets is known by such titles as *prepaid expenses, deferred charges, deferred charges to operations, deferred charges to expense, deferred expenses,* and *deferred assets.* Titles containing the words *deferred charges* may have a broader meaning than *prepaid expenses,* for they sometimes include additional items, such as discount on bonds payable. Prepaid expenses are treated as part of the current assets by many authorities. Others place them under a separate caption between the current and fixed groups. Still others place them as the last class of assets.

Fixed Assets are assets whose expected usefulness to the business will extend over several years. These assets are known by various terms, such as fixed, capital, permanent, and passive assets. They are more or less permanent but not necessarily immovable and do not vary in amount with small fluctuations in the volume of business. Fixed assets are kept as long as they serve the needs of the business. They are not purchased for resale because their absence would necessitate alteration of business policies, and they are difficult to convert into ready cash for the payment of debts. Fixed assets are not consumed entirely in one business operation, but as in the case of buildings, machinery, and other equipment, they wear out gradually. Both tangible and intangible assets may be included among the fixed assets, but some authorities place the intangibles in a separate group. Occasionally, intangibles and miscellaneous types of assets appear together under the caption *other assets*.

Current Liabilities are liabilities that mature within one operating cycle or one year, whichever is longer. They are referred to by such titles as current liabilities, working liabilities, floating liabilities, quick liabilities, and floating debt. Current liabilities usually include long-term liabilities that become due within a year of the date of the balance sheet. They are payable, ordinarily, out of current assets or by the creation of other current liabilities to replace them, such as the giving of a short-term note to pay an account payable that is due.

Income Received in Advance represents income received in one period but applicable to a subsequent period. This type of liability is known by such terms as *income received in advance, deferred credits to income, deferred credits, deferred income, deferred liabilities, deferred revenue, unearned income,* and *prepaid income*. The word *revenue* frequently appears in these titles instead of *income*. The term *credits* has a broader meaning than the other terms used here when it includes deferred credits to expense, such as premium received on bonds payable. The deferred credit, premium on bonds payable, is included properly with the long-term liabilities. Income received in advance is treated as a current liability by some authorities, and by others it is given a separate classification and placed either between current and long-term liabilities or as the last group of liabilities.

Long-Term Liabilities are liabilities that will not mature for a comparatively long time, usually more than a year. Long-term liabilities are also known as fixed liabilities, long-term obligations, long-term debt, and funded debt.

CHANGES IN BALANCE SHEET ITEMS

Transactions of a business cause increases and decreases in its assets, liabilities, and proprietorship.

Asset Changes. Assets are continually changing through (1) purchases or other acquisition, (2) fabrication in the manufacturing process, (3) conversion, (4) depreciation, and (5) sales or other disposition.

Liability Changes. Liabilities are continually changing through (1) additional purchases on credit, (2) borrowing, (3) paying off liabilities, and (4) exchanging one liability for another.

Proprietorship Changes. The proprietary interest is continually changing through (1) additional investments in the business, (2) profit or loss from operations, (3) gain or loss on nonoperating activities, and (4) withdrawals of earnings and investments.

CHAPTER 3

The Income Statement

Owners of a business enterprise normally wish to be informed about its progress from time to time. The three major financial statements designed to convey such information are: the balance sheet, discussed in the preceding chapter; the income statement, described in this chapter; and the statement of changes in financial position or funds statement, presented in Chapter 16.

INCOME

There are many interpretations of the term *income,* often called *revenue.* In accounting for a business, generally, the term *income* broadly applies to any increase in proprietorship other than additional investment by owners. Differences in the interpretation of income give rise to three principal definitions of the term, as follows:

1. Income is the exchange value of goods or services sold. It is variously termed *sales, gross sales, net sales, gross income from sales and services, gross income, revenue, gross revenue, gross receipts from operations, earnings,* and *gross earnings.*
2. Income is the difference between sales and cost of goods sold. This, in the opinion of many, is gross margin, gross margin on sales, gross profit, or gross profit on sales.
3. Income is the increase in proprietary interest resulting from any cause other than additional investment by the owners. Some authorities refer to this as net income, net profit, net gain, or net revenue.

Operating income has a somewhat restricted meaning; it is confined to income resulting from the rendering of services or the sale of goods in the primary operations of a business. *Primary operations* relate to those transactions that constitute the principal activities of an enterprise. Income, so defined, is gross income or operating gross income. All related operating costs and expenses must be subtracted from operating gross income to obtain the net operating income, net operating revenue, or operating profit.

Nonoperating income is income realized from sources not directly connected with the primary operations of a business. Extraordinary, nonrecurring items of a material amount should be segregated from the results of ordinary operations and shown separately on the income statement.

EXPENSES

Expenses refer to the cost of income or revenue gained or the outflow of commodities and services consumed in the operations of a business. As assets are consumed in business operations, their cost is said to expire. An expired cost is generally called an *expense*. Usage of the term expense indicates the following three concepts of its meaning:

1. Expense is the cost of obtaining income, as defined above.
2. Expense is sometimes defined more narrowly as the cost of commodities and services—other than the cost of goods sold—consumed in the operations of a business.
3. Expense, broadly defined, includes all items that decrease proprietorship, except capital withdrawals by the owners. This definition includes all expenses covered by the first definition and such items as income taxes (which may be considered to be a share of the profits taken by the government) and recorded extraordinary losses due to decreases in asset values resulting from fires, storms, market variations, and so on.

Operating expenses are expenses incurred in the primary operations of a business. *Nonoperating expenses* relate to operations other than the firm's primary operations. Some authorities treat all decreases in proprietorship except decreases resulting from the primary operations of the business and withdrawals of capital by the owners as nonoperating expenses.

Expense is sometimes confused with the terms cost, expenditure, disbursement, outlay, outgo, and loss. In order to avoid confusion, these terms are defined as follows:

1. *Cost* is the outlay made to acquire a commodity or service. The outlay may be in the form of cash, other assets, services, or the assumption of liability. The item acquired becomes an asset of the purchaser and is valued in the records, normally, at the acquisition cost. This cost is then assigned to the periods in which the asset produces benefits. The term *cost* is used loosely at times, as if it were identical in meaning with *expense*.

2. *Expenditure* is the outlay of money or services or the incurring of debt for any asset or expense. A more restricted concept of expenditure is that it represents cash payments. In this sense, it is synonymous with disbursement, outlay, and outgo.

3. *Disbursement, outlay*, and *outgo* are terms that refer to the payment of cash.

4. *Loss* is any decrease in the value of assets or any increase in liabilities for which no benefit is received. It is usually involuntary and irregular in occurrence. *Loss* is also used to refer to the excess of expenses over income. The term *net loss* is often used as the opposite of *net profit*. Certain items are labeled losses by some authorities, whereas others prefer to call them expenses. For example, ordinary losses on uncollectible accounts, claims from customers for shortages or damages, and the customary breakage and spoilage of goods in the process of manufacturing and handling represent a disappearance of values without a clearly discernible benefit. However, a business enterprise must assume a certain amount of risk if it extends credit to its customers and its manufacturing processes move with speed. It is customary, therefore, to consider such items as expenses because of their regular recurrence and prevalence in business. If they are extraordinarily large and irregular, they may properly be labeled losses.

THE STATEMENT

An *income statement* is a statement of the incomes and expenses of an individual or enterprise for a given period. The statement is known by a variety of titles, such as income statement, profit and loss statement, statement of income and expense, statement of operations, operating statement, income sheet, profit and loss account, income account, statement of loss and gain, revenue statement, statement of expense and revenue, statement of operating results, statement of income and capital account, statement of earnings, summary of income and expense, profit and loss summary, and trading, profit, and loss statement.

An income statement enumerates the amounts and the nature of incomes and expenses and the resulting difference, which is the net profit or loss for the period. This statement shows the results of operations for a period of time, known as an *accounting period* or a *fiscal period*, whereas the balance sheet shows the financial condition at a given date, and the funds statement reports the flow of funds during the accounting period.

Among financial reports, the income statement is considered second in importance only to the balance sheet. In a technical sense, it is a complementary statement, subordinate to the balance sheet; in reality, it is a part of the proprietorship section, which shows in greater detail how the proprietorship was changed during the accounting period. Nevertheless, the information on the income statement is of such great significance that both managers and owners of many enterprises consider the statement to be more important than the balance sheet.

Current Operating Statement. Formerly, most income statements were limited to reporting only income and expenses resulting from the ordinary, recurring operations of an entity during the current period. This type of report is known as a *current operating statement*. It is based on the *current operating performance concept*, which omits substantial extraordinary, nonrecurring gains and losses, such as those resulting from a sale of part of the enterprise and losses due to fire, flood, or other catastrophes. The extraordinary items are treated as direct additions to, or subtractions from, proprietorship.

Proponents of the current operating statement have argued that inclusion of extraordinary items in the income statement confuses many readers who are not readily able to distinguish between the results of the regular, recurring operations of the company, as a measure of its earning power, and the results of unusual circumstances.

All-Inclusive Income Statement. This form of income statement, recomended by the American Institute of Certified Public Accountants and widely adopted, includes all transactions causing changes in proprietorship during the current period, except substantial adjustments for prior periods and withdrawals and additional investments of owners. This type of report is known as an *all-inclusive income statement.* It is based on the *all-inclusive* or *clean surplus* theory. Substantial adjustments for prior periods, as well as withdrawals and additional investments by owners, are indicated in the proprietorship section of the balance sheet.

To be effective, the all-inclusive income statement must clearly indicate the net income from operations as an item separate and distinct from extraordinary gains and losses. The combined total of net income from operations and extraordinary gains and losses constitutes the net income for the period.

The term *clean surplus* refers to the fact that a corporation's *retained earnings* account, formerly known as *surplus,* will have total net income or loss recorded each year with only one adjustment when the all-inclusive income statement is used. On the other hand, if the current operating statement is preferred, perhaps numerous separate adjustments of retained earnings would be required for extraordinary items that are omitted from this type of income statement.

Supporters of the all-inclusive income statement contend that the income statement should report all incomes and expenses of the current period regardless of source and sometimes include adjustments of income of prior periods. As a result, the income statements of an enterprise would reveal the aggregate net income during the enterprise's lifetime.

Form of the Income Statement. Like the balance sheet, the income statement is not prepared according to a standard form. Two general types of forms are: the *account form*, sometimes called the *horizontal form*, and the *report form*, sometimes called the *vertical form* or *narrative form*.

1. *Account form.* An income statement is prepared in the account form by placing the cost of goods sold and expenses in a vertical column on the left side of the page and the incomes in a parallel column on the right side, as in an account. Equal totals are obtained by the balancing process. If it is desired to show cost of goods sold in greater detail, the opening inventories and purchases may be shown on the left side among the expenses and the closing inventories on the right side.

    In order to segregate types of operations and obtain desired subtotals, the various items may be classified into accounts, such as manufacturing, selling (trading), general and administrative (overhead), nonoperating, and perhaps, income taxes and appropriations.

    The account form of an income statement is technical. It is easily prepared by the accountant but not easily understood by a person unacquainted with bookkeeping techniques. At present, the account form is almost never used.

2. *Report form.* In this form, the items of income and expense are usually segregated into sections rather than accounts. Some of the sections commonly employed in a mercantile establishment are sales, cost of goods sold, operating expenses, nonoperating expenses, nonoperating income, and other income and expenses. Arrangement of items on the income statement of a typical mercantile company is described in the discussion of classification, on pages 25–30.

An income statement called the *single-step* form lists all income items in one group and all expenses in another and deducts total expenses from total income to arrive at net income. A single-step income statement is sometimes sufficient for the owners of a simple business enterprise, and it is used extensively, in a highly condensed form, in the published financial reports of large businesses.

Another type of income statement, the *multiple-step* form, also known as a *classified income statement*, contains several subsections and intermediate summary figures, which provide more details about the operations of an enterprise. Both single-step and multiple-step forms of income statement are practically always prepared in the report form.

Following are two illustrative income statements, one showing the single-step form and the other the multiple-step form. (Their net income figures appear in the proprietorship sections of the two illustrative balance sheets in Chapter 2, on pages 14 and 15. Appendix A presents an example of a manufacturing company's income statement on pages 220–221.)

CLASSIFICATION OF INCOME STATEMENT ITEMS

Generally, the income and expense items of all businesses are similar; but differences exist, especially among such organizations as a mercantile business, a manufacturing concern, an enterprise that renders personal services, and an enterprise that engages in more than one of these activities.

Classification of items of income and expense is a relative matter. For instance, expenses that can be classed as operating for one concern may be nonoperating expenses for another. The exact order of various items on the income statement may also vary, depending on the judgment of the accountant who pre-

McINERNY REAL ESTATE COMPANY

INCOME STATEMENT
FOR THE YEAR ENDED DECEMBER 31, 19--

Commissions earned		$51,640
Operating expenses		
Salaries and commissions expense	$22,370	
Office rent	2,400	
Office supplies and expense	1,290	
Telephone	480	
Automobile expense	1,120	
Depreciation of automobile	1,400	
Depreciation of office equipment	440	
Taxes and licenses	1,020	
Total operating expenses		30,520
Net income from operations		$21,120

COOK MERCANTILE COMPANY

INCOME STATEMENT
YEAR ENDED JANUARY 31, 19--

Revenue from sales			
Sales		$192,140	
Sales returns and allowances	$ 2,100		
Sales discounts	940	3,040	
Net sales			$189,100
Cost of goods sold			
Beginning inventory, February 1, 19--		$30,210	
Purchases	$118,920		
Purchase discounts	2,950		
Net purchases	$115,970		
Transportation in	4,940		
Delivered cost of purchases		120,910	
Cost of goods available for sale		$151,120	
Less ending inventory, January 31, 19--		32,430	
Cost of goods sold			118,690
Gross profit on sales			$ 70,410
Operating expenses			
Selling expenses			
Sales salaries and commissions	$ 36,760		
Delivery expenses	2,470		
Advertising	1,200		
Depreciation of store equipment	1,100		
Insurance	560		
Supplies	480		
Bad debts expense	300		
Miscellaneous	170		
Total selling expenses		$ 43,040	
Administrative and general expenses			
Office salaries	$ 7,350		
Taxes	2,860		
Depreciation of building	2,000		
Depreciation of office equipment	300		
Utilities	1,260		
Sundry office expenses	730		
Total general expenses		14,500	
Total operating expenses			57,540
Net income from operations			$ 12,870
Other income			
Rent income	$ 2,380		
Interest on investments	180	2,560	
Net income			$ 15,430

pares the statement. Following is a sectional classification of the income and expense items commonly found on the income statement of a mercantile company, together with various important computed totals.

Sales. This section shows the gross sales, sales returns, sales allowances, net sales, and, sometimes, sales discounts.

1. *Gross sales* include the total amount customers have paid or have agreed to pay for merchandise sold during the current accounting period. This term excludes sales of assets other than merchandise held for resale.

2. *Sales returns* represent sold merchandise that for any reason has been returned.

3. *Sales allowances* are deductions from the sales price to customers in lieu of the return of merchandise that is unsatisfactory.

4. *Sales discounts* are special discounts allowed customers for prompt payment. They are placed in this section by some authorities.

5. *Net sales* are computed by deducting from gross sales the sales returns, sales allowances, and sales discounts if included in this section.

Cost of Goods Sold. This section shows the beginning inventory, purchases, purchase returns, purchase allowances, purchase discounts (sometimes), net purchases, transportation in, delivered cost of purchases, cost of goods available for sale, the ending inventory, and cost of goods sold.

In a manufacturing enterprise, the statement of cost of goods manufactured and sold will include the above items but will deal with three inventories instead of one and will report such additional items as they relate to the manufacturing process. (Appendix A, page 221, gives an example.)

1. *Beginning inventory* represents the merchandise on hand at the beginning of the accounting period.

2. *Purchases* include the cost of merchandise acquired for resale during the accounting period. This term excludes acquisitions of assets other than merchandise purchased for resale.

3. *Purchase returns* represent merchandise that has been re-

turned for any reason to the vendors from whom it was purchased.

4. *Purchase allowances* are deductions from the purchase price obtained from vendors in lieu of the return of unsatisfactory merchandise to them.

5. *Purchase discounts* are special discounts received for prompt payment of invoices for merchandise purchases. They are placed in this section by some authorities.

6. *Net purchases* represent the amount obtained by deducting purchase returns, purchase allowances, and, sometimes, purchase discounts from the total amount of purchases.

7. *Transportation in,* or *freight and cartage in,* indicates transportation costs of merchandise purchased for resale.

8. *Delivered cost of purchases* includes the sum of net purchases and transportation in.

9. *Cost of goods available for sale* is the sum of the beginning inventory and the delivered cost of purchases.

10. *Ending inventory* represents the merchandise on hand at the end of the accounting period.

11. *Cost of goods sold* is obtained by subtracting the ending inventory from the cost of goods available for sale.

Gross Profit. This is a computed total obtained by subtracting cost of goods sold from net sales. Gross profit is also called gross profit on sales, gross trading profit, gross margin on sales, gross margin, and sometimes, as previously indicated, income or revenue.

Operating expenses. This section ordinarily is subdivided into selling expenses and general and administrative expenses.

1. *Selling expenses* include all expenses directly relating to the sale of merchandise. Some of the items ordinarily found in this group are as follows: sales salaries and commissions, delivery expense or cost of delivering merchandise sold, cost of storing merchandise awaiting sale, advertising, depreciation of sales equipment, insurance on merchandise and sales equipment, taxes and licenses applicable to sales, sales supplies used, miscellaneous selling expense, and, sometimes, bad debts expense.

2. *General and administrative expenses* include all operating expenses except those directly relating to the sale of mer-

chandise. Some of the items ordinarily found in this group are the following: office salaries, taxes and licenses, depreciation, telephone and telegraph, light and heat, rent, insurance, office supplies used, and miscellaneous office expense. Sometimes, bad debts expense, sales discounts, and interest expense are included in this section as financial management expense, which will be offset by financial management income such as purchase discounts and interest earned.

Operating Profit or Operating Loss. This is a computed total obtained by subtracting operating expenses from gross profit. If gross profit is greater than operating expenses, the difference is called *operating profit*. If operating expenses are greater than gross profit, the resulting figure is called *operating loss*. Various other titles for the difference between gross profit and operating expense include the following: net operating profit, net profit from operations, net income from operations, net operating revenue, net operating income, net operating gain, net gain from operations, net operating loss, and net loss from operations.

Nonoperating Income and Nonoperating Expenses. Nonoperating income and nonoperating expenses, previously defined, include income and expenses resulting from operations other than those for which the business was principally organized. At times, the nonoperating income and nonoperating expenses section of an income statement bears other titles such as other income and other expenses, outside income and outside expenses, financial and other income and expenses, and extraneous income and expenses.

1. *Nonoperating income* includes such items as rent received for a building not needed in the firm's own operations, interest on investments, interest on customers' notes, extraordinary and nonrecurring gains, and, sometimes, purchase discounts.
2. *Nonoperating expenses* include such items as interest on borrowed money, extraordinary expenses or losses, and, sometimes, sales discounts and bad debts expense.

Net Profit or Net Loss. Net profit or net loss is a computed total obtained by taking into consideration the operating profit or loss and the nonoperating income and expenses. If there is an operating profit, nonoperating income will be added and non-operating expenses will be subtracted to obtain net profit or loss. If there is an operating loss, nonoperating income will be subtracted and nonoperating expenses will be added to obtain net profit or loss. Instead of the separate addition or subtraction of nonoperating income and expenses, the difference between them is often added to, or subtracted from, operating profit or loss to obtain net profit or loss.

CHAPTER **4**

Accounts

BUSINESS TRANSACTIONS

Dual Elements in Every Transaction. A transaction, as previously defined, is an exchange of values. It is composed of two elements, both of which must be recorded in order to make a complete financial record. In any transaction, the presence of the dual elements is evident: in the fact that on one hand a commodity, right, or service is received, and on the other hand a commodity, right, or service is given up. An *exchange* has taken place.

A distinction is sometimes made between an *exchange* and a *conversion*. In a conversion, the dual elements of a transaction still appear; but the new commodity, right, or service results from the transformation of previously held commodities, rights, or services. However, an exchange and a conversion are similar in that one commodity, right, or service takes the place of another.

When the dual elements of a transaction are recorded, they cause increases and decreases in the assets, liabilities, and proprietorship of a business. For example, analysis will show that if a transaction results in an increase in an asset, there will be a corresponding decrease in another asset or an increase in either liabilities or proprietorship. This is only one of the various ways in which the balance sheet is affected by transactions.

Effects of Business Transactions on Financial Records. Every transaction involves one or more of the three balance sheet elements (assets, liabilities, and proprietorship) and causes increases and decreases in these elements. The effects of transac-

31

tions on the financial records, therefore, consist of asset changes, liability changes, and proprietorship changes, or combinations thereof. Any changes in the income and expense items are basically proprietorship changes, whose ultimate effects are reflected on the balance sheet.

Fundamental Types of Transactions. In terms of the balance sheet equation, there are only nine fundamental types of transactions. They are:

Asset increase accompanied by:
1. Asset decrease
2. Liability increase
3. Proprietorship increase.

Liability decrease accompanied by:
4. Asset decrease
5. Liability increase
6. Proprietorship increase.

Proprietorship decrease accompanied by:
7. Asset decrease
8. Liability increase
9. Proprietorship increase.

If liabilities and proprietorship are combined under the title equities, the nine fundamental types of transactions listed above can be restated as four types of transactions that have the same meaning. They are:
1. Equal increase and decrease in assets
2. Equal increase in assets and equities
3. Equal increase and decrease in equities
4. Equal decrease in assets and equities.

Every business transaction can be classified as one of the above types or a combination of them.

PHILOSOPHY OF DEBIT AND CREDIT

A system for recording business transactions should reveal the changes in assets, liabilities, and proprietorship with a minimum of space, effort, and error. Information should be available about each transaction that will precisely indicate what effect it has had on the balance sheet items. A more or less automatic proof of the accuracy of the resulting figures should also be provided. A poor accounting system will cause unnecessary work.

If a new balance sheet were prepared after each transaction, it would show the cumulative effects of the transactions and indicate the new total assets offset by the total amount of liabilities and proprietorship. Such a system would be extremely cumbersome, especially in a large business enterprise. However, a business executive does not want a complete new balance sheet after each transaction; because it would not show how the changes came about or provide the information necessary to construct the income statement. Greater efficiency is obtained by periodically analyzing the totals of some forms of transactions, such as sales, than by attempting to determine for each transaction what its full effect is on the balance sheet. Nevertheless, a record should be made promptly for each transaction.

Accounting techniques that provide brief and accurate methods of recording transactions have been developed. They separate the increases, or positive elements, from the decreases, or negative elements, relative to each account and then balance all asset accounts against all liability and proprietorship accounts.

One of the principles of debit and credit is that the elements comprising business transactions should be separated and classified and their combined results balanced in order to produce satisfactory business records efficiently.

Accounts. As discussed later in this chapter, *accounts* are a device used to record the effects of transactions on the assets, liabilities, and proprietorship of an enterprise. A business unit will use as many accounts, ordinarily, as it deems necessary to provide the detailed information it needs. The information given by these accounts is assembled periodically in the construction of a balance sheet and an income statement, supplemented perhaps by detailed schedules.

For convenience and uniformity, a conventional method of recording the balance sheet items in the accounts has generally been adopted. This method places additions to the assets on the left side of the accounts in which they are recorded and additions to the liabilities and proprietorship items on the right side of their accounts. (This arrangement is in harmony with the account form of a balance sheet, which places assets on the left side and liabilities and proprietorship on the right.) When an asset is increased as the result of a transaction, the amount of the increase is recorded in the asset account on the left side. When a liability or a proprietorship item is increased, the amount of the increase is placed in its account on the right side. Conversely, when an asset is decreased, the amount of the decrease is shown on the right side of the asset account; when a liability or a proprietorship item is decreased, the amount of the decrease is shown on the left side of the account that is affected.

In addition to the asset, liability, and proprietorship accounts, a number of temporary proprietorship accounts, or operating accounts, usually appear in the records under the classifications of income accounts and expense accounts. The operating accounts provide a record of a company's operations; the income accounts have the effect of increasing proprietorship and the expense accounts of decreasing proprietorship.

An Expanded Accounting Equation. The balance sheet equation given in Chapter 2 is reproduced here with the addition of income and expense accounts. This *expanded accounting equation,* sometimes called the *financial and operating equation,* illustrates with plus and minus signs the side of each class of accounts that contains increases and the side that contains decreases.

$$\text{Assets} = \text{Liabilities} + \text{Proprietorship} + \text{Income} - \text{Expense}$$
$$+\,|\,- \qquad -\,|\,+ \qquad -\,|\,+ \qquad -\,|\,+ \qquad +\,|\,-$$

DEBIT AND CREDIT

An understanding of the method of recording requires some familiarity with the terminology used by bookkeepers and accountants. Some of the terms have commonly been accepted and used in the business world for hundreds of years, even antedating the writings of Pacioli. Two terms are used in the recording process in connection with every business transaction; they are *debit* and *credit*. Custom has given conventional meanings to these words. Debit (abbreviated *Dr.*) refers to the left side of an account and credit (abbreviated *Cr.*) refers to the right side. When used as a noun, a debit is an entry on the left side and a credit is an entry on the right side of an account. As an adjective, the debit side of an account is the left side and the credit side is the right side. As a verb, to debit is to make an entry on the left side and to credit is to make an entry on the right side of an account. The word *charge* is frequently used instead of the word *debit*.

Remembering the debit and credit sides of an account, the increases and decreases shown in the expanded accounting equation can be summarized as follows:

Debit indicates:	*Credit* indicates:
Asset increase	Asset decrease
Liability decrease	Liability increase
Proprietorship decrease	Proprietorship increase
Income decrease	Income increase
Expense increase	Expense decrease

Since there is a dual aspect to each transaction, a complete record of a transaction requires that the total amounts of the debits and credits must be equal. This gives rise to a fundamental rule of accounting—for every debit there must be a credit. It is not necessary to have the same number of debit and credit items, but the debit and credit *amounts* must be equal.

DOUBLE-ENTRY BOOKKEEPING

Double-entry bookkeeping is the orderly recording of business transactions in financial terms in a manner that shows the effect of each transaction on the assets, liabilities, and proprietorship, and at the same time, maintains the equality of the total debits and credits. It is an effective and consistent system, of which an important part is the showing of the positive and negative elements relating to each item in separate columns. The double-entry system, though following established principles, has been revised to keep step with progress in modern enterprises.

SINGLE-ENTRY BOOKKEEPING

A method of financial record keeping that ignores the debit and credit elements involved is called *single-entry bookkeeping*. It lacks a journal and is based on memoranda such as check stubs, invoices, correspondence, and, perhaps, a listing of accounts receivable and accounts payable. It furnishes an incomplete record that makes the preparation of balance sheets and income statements difficult.

Single-entry bookkeeping is unsatisfactory for a business enterprise because of its incompleteness, but individuals whose financial operations are simple frequently depend upon sketchy memoranda and memory to supply the information needed for various purposes, such as preparation of income tax returns.

ACCOUNT FORM AND CONSTRUCTION

An *account* is a systematic arrangement of the increases and decreases of some specific asset, liability, or proprietorship item, or subdivision thereof, expressed in financial terms; such increases and decreases are usually segregated in parallel vertical columns.

An account, in a broad sense, is any device for recording the accumulated increases and decreases in an asset, a liability, or a proprietorship. This is true regardless of the form used. For instance, a checkbook in which the stubs show deposits and withdrawals of cash is a form of a cash account.

Structure of the Account. In its simplest form, an account may be shown as a *skeleton* account in order to save space and simplify the presentation of examples. The cash account, for instance, which has a balance of $900.00 may be presented as follows:

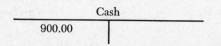

This is called a *T* account, because of its resemblance to a capital letter "T." The name of the account is placed at the top on the horizontal line. The vertical line separates the debits on the left from the credits on the right. This skeleton account form does not, however, give sufficient information for most bookkeeping purposes.

A more nearly complete example of the T account, which is widely used, supplies columns for additional data somewhat as follows:

Cash

19--							
Jan. 1	Balance		900.00				
(1)	(2)	(3)	(4)	(1)	(2)	(3)	(4)

This type of account is known as the *standard* account form. The columns provide space for the following information: (1) date of each entry, (2) necessary description or supplementary information, (3) folio or cross reference to indicate the page in another record on which a preliminary analysis of the transaction or transactions involved appears, and (4) amount.

Another widely used account form has only one date column, one explanation column, and one folio column, and the debit- and credit-amount columns are placed side by side at the right. In addition, there may be a column or two for the balance, the difference between the amount columns.

Many other forms of accounts are used. Specialized methods of recording, as with machines, have been the cause of numerous variations. Special types of information needed about some classes of transactions may make additional columns and special forms necessary.

Footing the Accounts. When the present status of an account is desired, it is ascertained by adding all the debit items and writing their total in small pencil figures below the last line used and by doing the same for the credit items. The difference between the total debits and the total credits, which is called the balance, is written in the description column of the larger side. The balance is a debit balance when the debit side is the larger and a credit balance when the credit side is the larger.

CLASSES OF ACCOUNTS

Accounts may be grouped into six principal classes, as follows:
1. Asset accounts
2. Liability accounts
3. Proprietorship accounts
4. Summarizing accounts
5. Income accounts
6. Expense accounts.

The asset, liability, proprietorship, income, and expense accounts contain the account elements suggested by their names. A *summarizing account,* known by such titles as *income summary, expense and revenue summary, profit and loss, profit and loss summary,* and *loss and gain accounts,* is used as a clearing account to which income and expense account balances are transferred at the end of an accounting period. The result of their combined balances is then transferred to the proprietorship accounts. Sometimes, additional summarization accounts are used, such as a cost of goods sold account or a manufacturing summary account.

There are many ways in which the accounts are grouped, depending upon the point of view. Sometimes, they are classified into the following four groups: assets, equities, income, and expense. When accounts are so grouped, the summarizing accounts are not included. The actual *elements* are then considered to be four in number, as indicated by the names of the four groups.

Real and Nominal Accounts. A convenient method of dividing the accounts into two groups is based on the financial statements. The asset, liability, and proprietorship accounts are labeled *real accounts,* and the income, expense, and summarizing accounts, *nominal accounts.*

Real accounts are also known as *balance sheet* or *permanent ac-*

counts. Nominal accounts are called *profit and loss, loss and gain, temporary, temporary proprietorship, intermediate, supplementary, ancillary, economic, explanatory, fictitious,* or *representative accounts.*

The real accounts represent items that are more or less permanent. Their balances at the end of one accounting period are retained as the balances at the beginning of the next period. The nominal accounts do not continue from year to year but are transferred to the proprietorship accounts periodically, usually as often as once a year. Seldom are such transfers made directly; they are usually made through the income summary account.

Mixed Accounts. At the close of an accounting period, some accounts commonly contain both real and nominal elements. These accounts are known as *mixed* accounts. The prepaid insurance account is an example. When a fire insurance premium is paid in advance, the amount becomes an asset representing a claim against the insurance company for the protection specified by the insurance policy. Later, a part of the prepaid insurance becomes insurance expense as the time passes that is covered by the policy. At the close of an accounting period, the amount of expired premium is recorded as an expense of the period, and the unexpired portion remains as an asset.

Suspense Account. Sometimes, the information available about a transaction is insufficient to complete the record at once, or an error may be discovered in the records that can be corrected more easily at a later date. Under such circumstances the questionable item may be placed in a suspense account until the necessary information is obtained. Accounts receivable and notes receivable whose collectibility is doubtful are sometimes recorded in suspense accounts. A suspense account may be used as a convenient, temporary expedient, but it should be used sparingly and, ordinarily, it should not be carried beyond the close of an accounting period.

Personal and Impersonal Accounts. A distinction is sometimes made between personal and impersonal accounts; *personal* refers to accounts with persons, and *impersonal* indicates all other accounts.

Permanent and Temporary Proprietorship Accounts. Income, expense, and summarizing accounts are in reality temporary proprietorship accounts, as already indicated. They contain information that could be recorded directly in the permanent proprietorship accounts, but a segregation is made into individual accounts to provide an analysis of the various kinds of income and expense. At the end of an accounting period, the temporary accounts customarily are closed directly or indirectly into the proprietorship accounts.

CHAPTER 5

The Ledger

A GROUP OF ACCOUNTS

The *ledger* is a group of accounts. It is a derived, or secondary, record presenting in analytical form the accumulated effects of transactions on the assets, liabilities, and proprietorship. Its sources of information are the books of original entry, called *journals*. Usually, only one account is placed on each page of the ledger.

Business practice formerly favored the use of bound books for the accounts, but the present tendency is to use loose-leaf forms printed on paper or cards or to use electronic equipment for financial record keeping. The bound ledger is inflexible in that new accounts or additional space for old accounts must be placed where blank pages are available. The increasingly popular loose-leaf ledger is more flexible and permits rearrangement of the accounts, if necessary. Sheets may be removed readily so that entries can be made with bookkeeping machines. New accounts can be placed where desired, and additional space can be given an account by simply inserting a new sheet along with the old. Furthermore, completely filled or dead sheets can be placed in a separate binder or transfer file for storage so that the current binder need not be unduly large.

CLASSIFICATION OF ACCOUNTS

Accounts usually are placed in a ledger and classified in some systematic manner. Even in a bound ledger, it is customary to

41

arrange the accounts in some definite order when they are first placed in the book. The order of their appearance will vary according to the needs and procedures of the business. The number of accounts will also vary, depending upon the amount of detail desired and the type of business.

Efficiency is promoted if care is used in planning the sequence of the accounts so that any desired account can be found quickly. Several methods are in general use.

Financial Statement Sequence is a popular plan for the arrangement of accounts. By placing the accounts in the ledger in the order of their appearance on the financial statements, a classification is obtained that groups the accounts according to types and simplifies preparation of the statements. An individual account can be located quickly by remembering its position on the balance sheet or income statement or by referring to a list or chart of the accounts.

Alphabetical Order is another arrangement that is sometimes used, especially when there are only a few accounts. Each account appears in alphabetical order according to the first significant word in its title, regardless of its position on the financial statements. Customers' accounts are frequently arranged in alphabetical order.

Other Sequences of accounts in the ledger are varied and depend on the type of business involved and the personnel of its accounting department. The accounts receivable may be arranged in a separate ledger according to their geographical locations if the management so desires.

Accounts are sometimes classified objectively (according to object or nature), so that there is an account for each general class or type of object for which the enterprise desires separate information. For instance, all of the machinery can be recorded in a machinery account, and all wages expense in one wages account. A more detailed classification is ordinarily required in order to provide a record according to departments or the functional organization of the enterprise. Such a classification by functions requires subdivision of the accounts relating to departmental activities so that results of the operations of each department can be determined separately.

CODIFICATION

Number and Letter Designations. Code numbers or letters, coordinated with the classification system, frequently serve to designate the various accounts. In a large enterprise, which requires a complex system of records and many accounts, there is need for some symbolic method of referring to the accounts in order to avoid constant repetition of the full descriptive titles. This saves time and saves space in some of the records where a cross reference to the accounts is needed. A small business may also find such symbols desirable, but the need for them is less urgent. Any system of codification must be planned with care to provide flexibility for normal expansion and minor changes in the classification.

Numerical Systems. These are widely used to identify accounts. The relationship of one account to another can be shown by combinations of numbers.

A typical numerical scheme assigns numbers to the principal groups of accounts in the following manner: assets, *1*; liabilities, *2*; proprietorship, *3*; summarizing account (income summary account), *4*; operating income, *5*; operating expense, *6*; and nonoperating income and nonoperating expense, *7*. The first digit of an account number indicates the group to which it belongs, and is repeated for each account in that group. Subsequent digits indicate subdivisions of that group.

Thus when the number *1* refers to all assets, the number *11* will refer to the current assets when they are listed as the first group of asset accounts. Then *111* will be the code number for cash as the first account among the current assets. If there are three cash accounts, the *111* will indicate their group location, and their individual numbers will be *111.1*, *111.2*, and *111.3*. Temporary investments, or marketable securities, will be numbered *112*, as the second type of accounts among the current assets; and receivables, as the third group, will be *113*. Notes receivable, the first account among the receivables, will be numbered *113.1*. Accounts receivable, as the next account, will be numbered *113.2*. If there are two accounts-receivable accounts, they will be numbered *113.21* and *113.22*. Next will be allowance for bad debts, or allowance for doubtful notes and accounts, a valuation account to be subtracted from total receivables and numbered *113V*. When the fixed assets are listed as the second major group of assets, their group number is *12* and the first account within the group is numbered *121*. A partial outline, or chart of accounts, for this numerical system follows:

1   Assets

11   Current assets

  111   Cash

    111.1   Petty cash

    111.2   Cash in bank

  112   Temporary investments

  113   Receivables

    113.1   Notes receivable

    113.2   Accounts receivable

      113.21   Accounts receivable, customers

      113.22   Accounts receivable, others

    113V   Allowance for bad debts (a valuation account)

  114   Inventories

  115   Prepaid expenses

12   Fixed assets

  121   Long-term investments

  122   Land

  123   Building

  123V   Allowance for depreciation of building (a valuation account)

This partial outline indicates how the Dewey decimal system is applied to the coding of accounts. The system can easily be adapted to fit a firm's individual needs. Other numerical systems use consecutive numbers for all accounts (in the order in which they appear in the ledger) and a variety of groupings of numbers.

Mnemonic Systems. These systems use code letters instead of figures to identify accounts. Key letters indicate the groups to which accounts belong, and other letters disclose the subclassifications within the groups. Combinations of letters and numbers are frequently used.

THE CHART OF ACCOUNTS

A chart showing the order in which the accounts are arranged is a convenient index to the ledger and an aid in the preparation of the financial statements. An example appears in Appendix A, pages 209–213. The chart of accounts is sometimes called a classification, schedule, table, card, or list of accounts. Such a chart can be used in a number of ways.

1. *An aid in system installation and revision.* When one is planning the installation of a new accounting system or the revision of an old one, it is desirable throughout the planning period to give serious thought to the accounts that will be needed by the enterprise. The effectiveness of the new records will greatly depend on the proper planning of the accounts. One of the early steps is the preparation of a tentative chart of accounts. If the accounting problems are complex, the chart may need constant attention and numerous revisions before plans for the new records are completed. The chart will then provide a guide for the preparation of the ledger by giving account titles and locations. It will also provide a summary, or bird's-eye view, of the accounts and a basis for the preparation of a manual of instructions, a book describing how the records are to be kept.

2. *An index to accounts used.* Regardless of the system followed in arranging the accounts in the ledger, it is desirable to have a chart of accounts, which serves as an index to the ledger. This not only enables the accounts to

be found readily, but is an aid in the preparation of entries, because it indicates the precise account titles or code designations to be used.

3. *A list of code numbers for ready reference.* When code numbers or symbols are used, they should appear on the chart of accounts with the full names of the accounts in order to provide a schedule for ready reference and thus facilitate the use of the code designations.

4. *An aid in using a uniform accounting system.* In several types of businesses, a uniform accounting system has been developed for the entire industry either by a regulatory body or by the industry voluntarily through its trade association. Where a uniform system is used, a complete chart of accounts is especially valuable as an aid to the intelligent operation of the system and the achievement of uniform results. The chart is useful for the reasons already outlined; it indicates the accounts that are authorized for the system and simplifies the use of the manual of instructions.

5. *An aid in preparing reports.* The preparation of financial reports is facilitated by the use of a chart of accounts, which indicates the names and locations of the accounts containing the information for such reports. This is of particular value when the accounts are arranged in statement order, because the classes and subclasses of accounts can then be indicated on the chart of accounts as they will appear on the reports. In some cases, the reports themselves indicate the numbers or symbols of the accounts that make up each item contained therein.

THE TRIAL BALANCE

A *trial balance* is a list of the ledger accounts at a specified date, showing their balances, or the debit and credit totals for each, in debit- and credit-amount columns. The totals of the two columns should be equal. When this is true, the ledger is said to be in balance.

The trial balance serves the following purposes:

1. It proves the equality of the total debits and credits in the ledger, thus providing at least a partial check on the accuracy of the bookkeeping.
2. It aids in detecting errors.
3. It furnishes a condensed picture of each account and a summary of all of the accounts.
4. It provides a basis for the preparation of the financial statements.

The trial balance is prepared periodically, usually at the end of each month. Either plain, ruled, or columnar paper is used. The trial balance requires at least three columns: the first for the account titles, the second for the debit amounts, and the third for the credit amounts. Ledger page numbers or account numbers are sometimes listed also.

Methods of Preparation. One of two methods is followed in showing the amounts opposite the respective account titles on the trial balance, as suggested in the definition above.

1. *Listing the balance of each account.* Many bookkeepers and accountants prefer to list only the balance of each account, placing all debit balances in the first amount column and all credit balances in the second. This requires less work than the alternate method, because fewer figures are listed and added. With this method, balances must be computed before the trial balance is taken, but they are used for the preparation of financial statements and must therefore be ascertained sooner or later in any event. Ordinarily, an account without a balance is not listed.
2. *Listing both debit and credit totals of each account.* The total of the debits for each account may be entered opposite the account title in the debit column, and the total of the credits, in the credit column. This method indicates the total amount, or volume, of the entries in each account instead of the difference between the debits and credits. Such information may be desired at times. Accounts that have debits and credits of the same amount are sometimes omitted from the trial balance, since the equality of the trial balance totals will not be affected either by the pres-

ence or the absence of the same amount in both the debit and credit columns.

Occasionally, a trial balance will combine the two methods described above by listing only the balances for some accounts and total debits and total credits for others.

Mistakes Not Disclosed by Trial Balance. The trial balance is a valuable accounting tool. It indicates that the debits and credits in the ledger are equal, which is necessary for a correct record, but it does not prove, thereby, that the books are entirely without error. Mistakes that the trial balance does not disclose may have occurred, such as:

1. *Compensating errors.* These are mathematical errors of the same amount, often called *counter errors,* which offset or neutralize each other. They may appear in both debit and credit columns or in one column only. Their presence in the trial balance may result from errors made in taking the trial balance or errors made in the books of original entry or in the ledger.

2. *Posting to wrong account.* An item may be posted, or entered, in the wrong ledger account although it is indicated properly in the journal, or book of original entry. This type of error, even if it is in the wrong account, will not disturb the equality of debits and credits if the amount appears on the proper side of the ledger.

3. *Incorrect classification in journal.* An erroneous classification of a transaction in a book of original entry will cause the information to be carried to the wrong account in the ledger.

4. *Transactions not recorded.* Whether or not a transaction appears in a book of original entry, if it is not recorded in the ledger, it will have no effect on the debits and credits of the accounts, and its absence will not be disclosed by the trial balance.

Cause of Unequal Trial Balance Totals. If a trial balance is out of balance, the difference between the totals is caused by one or more mistakes. Such errors may have occurred in the trial balance, the ledger, or the books of original entry. They can be classified as follows:

1. *Errors in addition or subtraction.* Any error in computing

totals or balances in the records will disturb the equilibrium of the debits and credits, unless it is neutralized by one or more compensating errors.

2. *Listing figures on wrong side of an account.* If a debit is shown on the credit side of an account or a credit on the debit side, there will be a discrepancy between the trial balance totals, unless it is offset by other errors.

3. *Listing incorrect figures.* The trial balance may not balance because an amount has been copied incorrectly. This type of error is likely to occur in one of the following ways:

    a. *Duplicate posting of a debit or credit.* Two entries may be made for one debit or credit amount.

    b. *Incorrect copying of one or more digits.* An amount may be inaccurate because one or more of its digits is written incorrectly.

    c. *Transposition of figures.* Digits may be transposed when an amount is being copied. An 87 may be written 78, or 162 may appear as 261.

    d. *Transplacement of figures.* Any of the digits of a number may be moved one or more spaces to the right or left, making a transplacement, or slide, as when 87 is written 870 or 8.70 or 800.70.

4. *Omission of amounts.* An amount may be omitted entirely, causing the records to be out of balance.

CHAPTER **6**

The Journal and
Bookkeeping Procedures

PRELIMINARY RECORDS

Ledger an Incomplete Record. A business enterprise needs a ledger to provide a cumulative analysis of the effects of its transactions, but the use of a ledger alone is not satisfactory. Although it is possible to record transactions directly in the ledger accounts, such procedure is usually inadvisable. It fails to meet all of the requirements of a complete accounting system. Various reasons why the ledger is an incomplete record are as follows:

1. *Chronological history not available.* A business enterprise should keep a chronological record of its transactions in order to simplify references made to its activities according to date. Ledger accounts do not provide such a record; therefore, when only a ledger is used, there is no day-to-day history of the business.

2. *Information disconnected.* Ordinarily, each transaction affects more than one account. When the debits and credits necessary to record a transaction are entered in the accounts, they become separated and the complete transaction is not shown in one place.

3. *Details inadequate.* Only meager information concerning a transaction can be shown conveniently in the account.

4. *Division of labor hampered.* Only one person at a time can make entries efficiently in the ledger. He must have the entire ledger available in order to record the transactions in each account affected. A large enterprise, with a multitude of transactions to record, must use a more effective

system. Its recording process must permit many employees to work on the books at the same time.

5. *Errors difficult to locate.* Making the entries directly in the ledger increases the probability that errors will occur and makes errors more difficult to locate and correct. The following are examples:

   a. Omitting one part of a transaction
   b. Entering part of a transaction on the wrong side of an account
   c. Entering the wrong amount in an account
   d. Entering an amount in the wrong account.

These possibilities make it desirable to have an accounting system that contains a preliminary record where the transactions will be shown in chronological order, complete in one place, and with adequate explanations as to their nature.

THE JOURNAL

The *journal* is a book of original entry in which transactions are recorded in their chronological order, showing a date for each, amounts and accounts to be debited and credited, and an explanation. The journal may also be a file of documents, punched cards, reels of punched or magnetic tape, or other media. The journal is considered the book of first entry although its entries are often based on memoranda that are previously prepared in auxiliary records, in which the details of the transactions are given. Outstanding features of the journal are as follows:

1. *A chronological record.* A day-by-day history of the transactions of the enterprise is provided.
2. *A debit and credit analysis of transactions.* Each transaction must be analyzed to ascertain its debit and credit elements when it is recorded in the journal. The journal analysis provides the information needed in the ledger.
3. *A brief explanation of each transaction.* Not all transactions require an extensive explanation in the books, but there should be enough detail in the explanation to help recall the essential features.

Form of General Journal. Any business transaction can be recorded in a simple journal. An enterprise may use several journals in which to record special phases of its activities, but it will ordinarily need one additional journal for miscellaneous entries, known as the *general journal,* and sometimes referred to merely as the *journal.* Its form characteristically embodies two amount columns at the right, one for debits and the other for credits. An illustration follows.

Journal

(1)	(2)	(3)	(4)	(5)

The columns provide space for the following information: (1) date, (2) account title and explanation, (3) ledger folio— L. F., (4) debit amount, and (5) credit amount. This is a standard form for the general journal and is widely used, although variations are employed. Some enterprises find that the efficiency of the general journal is improved by the use of more than two amount columns; the additional columns provide space in which to enter debits and credits that occur frequently enough to make their segregation in special columns desirable. Chapter 10 discusses special columns and special journals.

JOURNALIZING

Recording transactions in a journal is known as *journalizing.* Before a transaction can be recorded in a journal, it must be analyzed to determine what accounts should be debited and what accounts should be credited. The general concept of the term *journalizing* includes: (1) the preliminary analysis of the transaction and (2) the actual recording in the journal.

The record of a transaction in a journal is called a *journal entry.* Ordinarily, a journal entry relates to one transaction, but it can be used to record a group of transactions. A complete journal entry contains equal debit and credit amounts, following the fundamental rule of accounting—for every debit there must be a credit.

Content of the Journal Entry. Each entry in the two-column journal normally contains the following six parts:

1. *Date.* The date of the transaction to be recorded is placed in the date column at the left side of the journal page on the line used for the first debit item. The year should be shown at the top of the page. When two date columns are used, the name of the month is placed in one and the day of the month in the other. Frequently, the name of the month is omitted from all but the first entry on a page. The date may be placed at the middle of the journal page on the line immediately above each entry, showing either the month, day, and year, or the day only, with the month and year written at the top of the page. It is customary to leave one or two blank lines between entries in the general journal, but no blank lines within an entry, so that the record of each transaction is clearly distinguishable.

2. *Titles of accounts to be debited.* The title of each account to be debited is written on a separate line in the column used for account titles and explanation, starting at the left edge of that column. The accounts named in a journal entry indicate the ledger accounts affected by the entry. Care should be exercised so that the exact account titles used in the ledger appear in the journal. This helps to find the right account in the ledger quickly and to avoid confusion when the names of accounts are somewhat similar. Debits usually precede credits in a general journal entry.

3. *Debit amounts.* Any debit amounts relating to the transaction are entered in the left-hand amount column opposite their respective account titles.

4. *Titles of accounts to be credited.* The title of each account to be credited is written in the account and explanation column, uniformly indented from the left edge, and beginning on the line immediately following the last debit item.

5. *Credit amounts.* Any credit amounts relating to the transaction are entered in the right-hand amount column opposite their respective account titles.

6. *Explanation.* An entry in the general journal should usually include an explanation. Customarily, the explanation is brief, but it should be sufficient to help recall full particu-

lars. There is no standard form for this entry, but many bookkeepers start the explanation on the line immediately following the last credit item, and write only in the account and explanation column.

Simple and Compound Journal Entries. In a journal, an entry that contains only one debit item and one credit item is called a *simple journal entry*. If more than one debit and one credit are necessary, the entry is a *compound journal entry*. Following is an example of a simple journal entry, made on September 1, and a compound journal entry, made on September 2:

Journal

19- -			
Sept. 1	Cash	30,000.00	
	J. Jones, Proprietorship		30,000.00
	Invested cash for the purpose of establishing the Jones Hardware Store		
2	Land	4,000.00	
	Building	14,000.00	
	Furniture and Fixtures	2,000.00	
	Cash		20,000.00
	To record purchase of land, building, and fixtures for cash		

POSTING

Transferring debit and credit items listed in a journal to their respective accounts in a ledger is called *posting*.

Each debit item in an ordinary two-column journal is posted to the ledger by entering in the debit column of the proper account the amount shown in the debit column of the journal opposite that account title. Each credit item is posted by entering in the credit column of the proper account the amount shown in the credit column of the journal opposite that account title. In the process of posting, the debit and credit items are taken in any order desired. For instance, all debits may be posted before the credits. Many bookkeepers see no advantage in this method, however, and prefer to post the items in the order of their appearance in the journal.

As each item is posted, the number of the ledger account (or the page number) to which it is posted is entered in the folio column of the journal on the line on which the item appears. At the same time, the page number of the journal is placed in the folio column of the ledger account on the line on which the item is posted. This is sometimes called *paging*. The folio columns thus provide a cross reference, which simplifies the tracing of entries, and also shows whether or not an item has been posted. Check marks sometimes are used instead of numbers, especially if neither the accounts nor the ledger pages are numbered. Either check marks or numbers should be placed in the journal folio column at the time of posting so that blank spaces in the column will indicate what items are still to be posted. Some bookkeepers enter the account numbers with the account titles when making a journal entry, and place a check mark beside each amount in the journal when it is posted.

RELATION BETWEEN JOURNAL AND LEDGER

The journal and the ledger are the basic books of a double-entry accounting system. Both books are essential to a complete and efficient accounting system. The journal is the chronological record, and the ledger is the analytical record. The journal is the book of original entry; the ledger is the book of second entry, a derived record. The journal, as a book of first entry, ordinarily has greater weight as legal evidence than the ledger.

CHAPTER 7

Periodic Adjustments
and Summarization

CASH AND ACCRUAL BASES OF ACCOUNTING

Cash Basis. If the *cash basis* is used in keeping the books, income is recorded only when cash is received and expense is recognized only when cash is paid out.

The cash basis is often modified to include the recording of accounts payable, accounts receivable, and depreciation. If depreciation is recognized, it is computed periodically in the same manner as if the business were on the accrual basis. An enterprise that has a merchandise inventory cannot ordinarily operate effectively on the cash basis.

The cash method of accounting is frequently used by professional people, nonprofit organizations, and small businesses and by individuals for personal and family records.

Accrual Basis. The *accrual basis* offers a more accurate method of acounting than the cash basis. When the *accrual basis* is used, income is recorded for the fiscal period in which it is earned, whether or not it is received during that period. Expenses incurred in earning the income are recorded as expense, whether or not payment has been made for them during that period. The resulting income statement includes only the income that was earned and the expenses that were incurred during the period covered by the statement.

Determining the date on which income is actually earned and properly allocating expenses to that income sometimes present difficulties. Solutions of such problems generally require consideration of all the known factors. When the accrual basis is employed, the financial statements usually cannot be prepared until adjustments have been made for accrued and prepaid items. Complete and accurate balance sheets and income statements depend upon the inclusion of various income and expense items that have accrued from day to day and have not been recorded currently in the accounts. It is not practicable to record this information daily, because some necessary information is not available, except at longer intervals. Also, it is not necessary to make daily changes, since the complete information is customarily needed only at the end of the accounting period.

THE ACCOUNTING PERIOD

The period of time that is covered by an income statement, or the time that has elapsed between successive balance sheets, is the *accounting period*. It is also called the *fiscal period*. Enterprises ordinarily have an accounting period of one year, which frequently coincides with the calendar year. Many businesses, however, have found that there are advantages in using a *natural business year*, which ends on the last day of a month other than December.

The natural business year chosen begins and ends when the regular annual cycle of business activities of a concern is at its lowest point; for example, most department stores close their books and make their annual reports on January 31, during the relatively quiet period following the rush of Christmas business and January clearance sales.

A large enterprise will usually divide its fiscal year into other accounting periods, so that in addition to the annual financial statements, the firm will prepare more frequent reports, such as semiannual, quarterly, and monthly reports.

INTERIM STATEMENTS

Managements of large enterprises generally require financial statements more often than once a year in order to provide information about current operations. The statements can be prepared as often as is necessary with the aid of work sheets, described in this chapter, and without closing the books until the end of the fiscal year. Such statements are known as *interim statements*. Monthly income statements frequently contain comparable figures from the preceding month, and perhaps, from the same month of the preceding year, together with up-to-date totals for the current year.

TYPES OF ACCRUED AND DEFERRED ITEMS

Use of the accrual method of accounting gives rise to a number of accrued and deferred items. Their existence is due to the many income and expense transactions that relate to more than one period. Some of these items are discussed in later chapters. The groups into which they are classified are as follows:

1. *Accrued income* is income earned for which payment is not due to be received until a subsequent period or periods.
2. *Accrued expense* is an expense of the present period for which payment is due to be made in a subsequent period.
3. *Deferred income* is income received but not yet earned.
4. *Deferred expense* represents commodities or services purchased for use in the business but not consumed at the end of the accounting period.

ADJUSTMENTS

Adjusting Entries. An adjusting entry may be made at any time that an account needs adjustment. The term *adjusting entries*, however, refers particularly to the periodic entries made at the close of an accounting period to bring the ledger accounts up to date. Mixed accounts are adjusted in order to separate the real from the nominal elements. Every adjusting entry involves at least one real account and at least one nominal account.

Common Types of Adjustments. There are four common types of adjustments. These adjustments are discussed in detail in the next two chapters. The four types are classified as follows:

1. *Merchandise inventory*
2. *Accrued and deferred items*
3. *Depreciation*
4. *Bad debts.*

Correcting Entries. A distinction is sometimes made between adjusting entries, discussed above, and correcting entries. When errors are discovered in the accounts, they may be rectified through the use of correcting entries. Such entries should ordinarily be made when the errors are found, whether within the accounting period, at the close of the period, or at a subsequent time.

THE WORK SHEET

A *work sheet,* or *working sheet,* is a columnar device that readily enables the unadjusted account balances shown in the trial balance to be adjusted and segregated into balance sheet and income statement items. The work sheet is an accountant's tool used to facilitate preparation of the periodic financial statements. The accountant therefore uses any one of the various forms available, whichever is best suited to his needs.

One form of a ten-column work sheet is as follows:

Name of Account	Trial Balance		Adjustments		Adjusted Trial Balance		Income Statement		Balance Sheet	
	Dr.	Cr.	Dr.	Cr.	Dr.	Cr.	Dr.	Cr.	Dr.	Cr.

Steps in Preparation of a Ten-Column Work Sheet. The following are steps in the preparation of one type of the ten-column work sheet.

1. In the trial balance columns, enter the balances of the

ledger accounts as they appear before the adjusting and closing entries are made. Add the debit and credit columns, which must have equal totals.

2. In the adjustments columns, enter all adjusting entries.

3. In the adjusted trial balance columns, extend the trial balance, giving effect to the adjustments, and foot the columns.

4. Distribute the adjusted trial balance figures by placing the income and expense items in the income statement columns and the asset, liability, and proprietorship items in the balance sheet columns.

5. Foot the income statement and balance sheet columns, using one horizontal line. On the next line, enter the balancing figure under the smaller of the two totals in the income statement columns and also under the smaller total in the balance sheet columns. The same amount, representing either net income or net loss for the period, should balance the four columns. If the amount is in the income statement debit column and the balance sheet credit column, it represents a net profit and is so labeled on the same line in the first, or name, column. A net loss for the period is indicated when the balancing figure appears in the income statement credit column and the balance sheet debit column, and it is so labeled on the same line in the first, or name, column. The next line, for totals, shows that the totals of the two income statement columns agree and the totals of the two balance sheet columns agree. An example of an eight-column work sheet appears in Appendix A, pages 215 and 216.

Variations in the Work Sheet Columns. Work sheets may have more or fewer columns than the ten-column work sheet illustrated above.

1. The *eight-column* work sheet omits the adjusted trial balance columns. It is frequently used by accountants, because it distributes the adjusted account balances directly to the income statement and balance sheet columns without the extra work of entering them first in the adjusted trial balance columns.

2. The *six-column* work sheet omits the adjustments columns; it is not frequently used.

3. The *twelve-column* work sheet for a mercantile concern may include a pair of columns for additional information, such as trading account, cost of sales, cost of goods sold, or retained earnings.

4. *Multi-column* work sheets, including ten, twelve, or more columns, are frequently used by manufacturing concerns and occasionally by mercantile concerns.

Effects Achieved by the Work Sheet are indicated by this list of its purposes, uses, and advantages:

1. The usual form of trial balance is provided to determine whether the debits and credits in the ledger are equal.

2. A summary of the accounts is provided, which shows the results of the fiscal period and gives the accountant a panoramic view of the enterprise.

3. Reference to previous work sheets helps the accountant to plan the work for the close of the accounting period and facilitates adjustment and closing of the books.

4. Adjustments of accounts for inventories, accruals, etc., are made tentatively, and their accuracy is proved before they are actually entered in the journal and the ledger.

5. The mathematical accuracy of entries, accounts, and statements is known before the books are closed.

6. The profit or loss for the accounting period is quickly ascertained, in fact, even before the books are adjusted and closed or the statements are prepared.

7. The work sheet usually supplies the information necessary for the preparation of the formal adjusting and closing entries.

8. Classification and segregation of assets, liabilities, incomes, and expenses are provided.

9. Preparation of financial statements is facilitated by the work sheet. In fact, the statements are usually prepared from the work sheet before the adjusting and closing entries have been placed in the books.

10. Interim statements may be prepared at intervals without formally closing the books.

CLOSING ENTRIES

Closing entries are periodic entries made at the end of an accounting period to close the temporary proprietorship accounts, consisting of the income, expense, and summarizing accounts. These entries are made to segregate and summarize the incomes and expenses for each fiscal period so that the net gain or loss for the period can be determined.

The income statement can be used as a guide when preparing the closing entries, but more often these entries are based on the income statement columns of the work sheet, as mentioned above.

The closing entries serve a twofold purpose:

1. They clear the nominal accounts covering the transactions of the past fiscal period.
2. They show, in the proper proprietorship accounts, the net effects of all operations of the fiscal period.

Closing entries are entries used to transfer the balances of the nominal, or temporary proprietorship, accounts to proprietorship. This is usually done by means of an intermediate summarization account, or clearing account–income summary.

Closing entries are usually made in two distinct steps. The first step is to close all open income and expense accounts to the income summary account. The second step is to close the income summary account to proprietorship.

BALANCING AND RULING THE ACCOUNTS

Asset, liability, and proprietorship accounts that have a larger total amount in one column than the other at the close of the fiscal period are balanced by writing the word *Balance* in the description column of the smaller side, usually on the first available line, and entering the amount of the difference between the pencil footings of the two previously computed columns in the money column. Now, the debit and credit totals are equal. A single line is then drawn across both amount columns on the same horizontal line just below the lowest debit or credit amount, and the identical totals of the two columns are written on the next line. A double ruling follows; it is placed immediately below the totals and sometimes across all columns except the explanation or description columns. Below the double ruling, on what was the larger side, the date is entered, the word *Balance* is written in the description column, and the amount of the difference, or balance, is written in the money column.

All accounts that do not have a balance remaining at the end of the fiscal period are totaled and double ruled underneath the totals. If there is only one entry on each side of an account and they are for equal amounts, the double ruling is usually considered to be sufficient.

POST-CLOSING TRIAL BALANCE

A trial balance of the ledger is often taken after all adjusting and closing entries have been journalized and posted and the accounts have been balanced and ruled. Such a trial balance is termed the *post-closing trial balance*. This is done to verify the accuracy of the work and to show that the ledger is in balance at the beginning of the next accounting period. The post-closing trial balance can also be checked against the balance sheet columns of the work sheet and the formal balance sheet for verification.

REVERSING ENTRIES

After the ledger has been closed, the balances of the accounts representing accrued and deferred items, which consist of accrued expenses, deferred charges to expense, accrued income, and deferred credits to income, remain on the books as assets and liabilities. A customary procedure is to transfer them to the respective income and expense accounts to which they relate and from which they came. Transferring entries, ordinarily termed *reversing, reversal, readjusting,* or *post-closing* entries, are made in the general journal. They are usually entered before the ordinary business transactions of the new fiscal period, but they may be delayed until the close of the fiscal period.

An alternative procedure, which avoids the use of reversing entries, is to close the accrued and deferred accounts when transactions occur to which they relate. Reversing entries are sometimes discussed along with the closing entries, since they are a part of the periodic adjustment and summarization process.

THE ACCOUNTING CYCLE

The *accounting cycle*, or *bookkeeping cycle*, as discussed so far, contains the following steps:

1. Journalize the ordinary business transactions.
2. Post.
3. Foot the accounts and take the trial balance.
4. Determine the adjustments, such as inventories, accruals, etc.
5. Complete the work sheet.
6. Prepare the financial statements and schedules.
7. Journalize and post the adjusting entries.
8. Journalize and post the closing entries.
9. Balance and rule the accounts.
10. Take post-closing trial balance.

CHAPTER 8

The Merchandise Inventory

Business enterprises engaged in selling merchandise that they have either manufactured or purchased for resale generally have an important part of their resources invested in such goods, called the *merchandise inventory*. The value of the goods on hand must be ascertained from time to time to compute the owner's profit or loss from operations.

TAKING INVENTORY

Taking inventory, or counting the merchandise on hand, usually occurs at regular intervals, at least as often as once a year and preferably at or near the close of the annual accounting period. Enterprises that require frequent financial statements generally adopt some method of computing or estimating the inventory and then check on its accuracy occasionally, perhaps annually, by actually counting the merchandise on hand. There are two principal methods of accounting for inventories: periodic and perpetual.

THE PERIODIC INVENTORY

The *periodic*, or *physical*, inventory method is used by most small businesses and many large ones. It is simple and usually sufficient for an enterprise that can wait until the inventory has been taken to have its financial statements prepared. It requires an actual count of the merchandise on hand, generally at the end of each annual accounting period. The amount so determined is carried in the merchandise inventory account and is not changed until the close of the succeeding period, when the account is adjusted to show the amount of the new inventory.

There are various ways of adjusting the merchandise inventory account, of which the following three are representative:

1. *Adjustment through income summary account.* With this method, the amount in the old merchandise inventory account is transferred to the income summary account by the following journal entry:

Income Summary

Merchandise Inventory

The amount of the new inventory is then recorded by this entry:

Merchandise Inventory

Income Summary

The merchandise inventory and income summary accounts appear like this:

Merchandise Inventory

Inventory (old)	Inventory (old)
Inventory (new)	

Income Summary

Inventory (old)	Inventory (new)

The purchases account and the other accounts relating to merchandise are closed to the income summary account.

This method of adjusting the merchandise inventory account is used frequently, especially in small businesses. Its use is particularly advantageous in that (1) the same form may be used regardless of the comparative sizes of the old inventory, the new inventory, and purchases and (2) all the detailed information needed for the preparation of the income statement is available in one place—the income summary account. Some authorities prefer to accomplish the same results by making these entries closing rather than adjusting entries.

2. *Adjustment through cost of goods sold account.* The cost of goods sold account is another summarization account used by accountants in the adjustment of the merchandise inventory account. When the cost of goods sold account is used, several variations in entries are employed, but one typical way can illustrate its use. The old inventory figure is closed by an entry such as:

> Cost of Goods Sold
> Merchandise Inventory

The new inventory figure is recorded by this entry:

> Merchandise Inventory
> Cost of Goods Sold

The balances of purchases and related accounts are transferred to the cost of goods sold account by entries such as:

> Cost of Goods Sold
> Purchases
> Freight In

and:

> Purchase Returns
> Purchase Allowances
> Cost of Goods Sold

The cost of goods sold account is closed to the income summary account by one of the closing entries.

Although this method of adjusting merchandise inventory does not give the detailed information in one place that is needed to prepare the income statement, it does provide a summary of the cost of goods sold, which would otherwise be available only in the income statement.

3. *Adjustment through purchases account.* The purchases account can be used as a summarization account in a third method of adjusting the merchandise inventory account. In such instances, the purchases account resembles the cost of goods sold account. The old inventory is closed to it, the new inventory is set up out of it, and the various related accounts are closed into it. The balance of the purchases account is then the cost of goods sold and is closed into the income summary account by one of the closing entries.

This is only one of the various ways in which the purchases account can be utilized in adjusting the merchandise inventory account.

THE PERPETUAL INVENTORY

The *perpetual,* or *continuous,* inventory method necessitates keeping a continuous record of all goods on hand. Thus, an additional entry is required when each sale is made. A cash purchase is recorded as follows:

Merchandise
Cash

When a cash sale is made, the usual entry is:

Cash
Sales

This is accompanied by the following entry, the amounts being the cost price of the goods sold:

Cost of Goods Sold
Merchandise

When these entries have been posted to the ledger, the accounts affecting merchandise appear as follows:

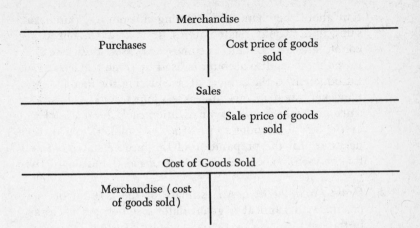

After the merchandise account has been debited for the purchases and credited for the cost of goods sold, the balance remaining purports to be the cost of the merchandise on hand. Since this does not take into consideration merchandise that has been destroyed, damaged, or stolen, a periodic, or physical, inventory should be taken at least annually; and the merchandise account should be adjusted. There are variations in the method of recording the perpetual inventory, and additional techniques are often employed, including the use of punched cards and electronic computers.

A perpetual inventory system is not satisfactory for some merchandising concerns, since the physical inventory must still be taken and the cost of goods sold is often difficult to compute for each transaction. Many manufacturing concerns, however, have found that the maintenance of perpetual inventory records improves their efficiency and saves money.

OTHER INVENTORY PROCEDURES

Three additional variations in accounting for merchandise inventory should be noted.

1. *Mixed merchandise account.* A single mixed merchandise account is sometimes used to supply the desired informa-

tion about merchandise, including inventories, purchases, sales, and various related items. It is called a mixed account, since it contains incomes, expenses, and assets. A mixed merchandise account is used by some teachers as an introduction to the subject of accounting for merchandise. However, such an account is seldom found in business, since an analysis and summarization must be made of the entries in the account to provide the detailed information necessary for the preparation of the income statement and for the use of executives in charge of merchandising activities.

2. *Gross profit method.* An estimate of the amount of merchandise on hand at a given date is sometimes necessary in the absence of a perpetual inventory system. For example, the amount of merchandise lost in the event of fire or burglary usually must be estimated. An estimate is also needed for the completion of the financial statements when statements are required more frequently than the periodic physical count of the merchandise on hand.

An enterprise whose ratio of gross profit to sales is accurately computed and relatively steady can estimate gross profit based on this ratio and thus make a reasonably close estimate of the amount of merchandise inventory. Such a method is not ordinarily intended to supplant one of the other methods but only to supplement its usefulness.

3. *Retail inventory method.* Widely adopted by large department stores, the retail inventory method provides an acceptable way of computing the amount of the merchandise inventory. Its accuracy is tested from time to time by making a physical count of the stock on hand. Whereas the gross profit method depends on the ratio of gross profit to sales experienced in past periods, the retail inventory method utilizes the ratio of cost to selling price of the merchandise available for sale during the current period.

Under the retail method, the opening inventory and all purchases and purchase returns are recorded at both cost and selling prices, and a careful record is maintained of all later increases in the selling price, or markups, and all decreases, or markdowns. The ratio of cost to selling price is then computed for the total goods available for sale.

The amount of merchandise on hand in a department at any time can be readily determined by subtracting total sales of the department from the retail value of the opening inventory plus purchases at selling prices and adjusting for additional markups, markdowns, freight in, and, perhaps, estimated loss from pilferage or other shrinkage. The retail value of the resulting inventory is converted to approximate cost by applying the ratio of the cost of merchandise available for sale during the current period to the selling price of the same merchandise.

The retail method helps to maintain control over inventories, because with this method, careful records must be kept and a simple formula is used to compute the amount of merchandise on hand at any date without a physical count. When the actual count is made, periodically, it is expedited by listing the articles at the retail prices marked on them and then converting the total amount to cost. In order for the retail method to be effective, the goods included in one computation must have a fairly uniform rate of markup. Consequently, a store usually has several groupings of merchandise with different markups.

Adjustment of the merchandise inventory account is a necessary step in the allocation of costs. The allocation must be extended to supplies and other costs that are only partially consumed in a single accounting period in order to obtain total expense figures that are as accurate as possible. This is true in a mercantile establishment and is even more evident in accounting for the goods being produced by a manufacturing enterprise.

A manufacturer typically needs three merchandise inventory accounts, instead of the one that is sufficient for a merchant. The three accounts are: *raw materials*, or *materials; goods in process*, or *work in process;* and *finished goods*. These accounts will be discussed in greater detail in a subsequent chapter.

VALUATION OF INVENTORIES

Inventory Pricing. Cost of the merchandise inventory consists of the purchase price and all additional expenditures necessary to make the goods available for sale, including such costs as transportation, duties, and insurance. The amount of inventory on hand often is one of the largest assets on a company's balance sheet, and the cost of merchandise sold almost always is the largest single cost item on its income statement. A slight variation in the plan for valuing a large inventory can make a substantial difference in the inventory total and the resulting computation of profit. The pricing plan adopted should produce an acceptable valuation of the goods on hand and should consistently be followed to facilitate comparisons of performance from period to period. Following are the types of inventory valuation most frequently encountered:

1. *Specific identification.* If the cost of the specific goods on hand can readily be determined, there is justification for using the *identifiable unit cost* basis in the valuation of the inventory. For example, a dealer can follow this plan if he marks cost (preferably in code), as well as selling price, on his merchandise or if his inventory consists of relatively few expensive units, such as pianos or automobiles, whose individual costs can be ascertained from supplementary records. The plan is not feasible when units of fungible merchandise, purchased at various prices, are intermingled and lose their identity, as happens when a gasoline dealer places his purchases in a single tank. In situations where individual units cannot be identified or where the clerical effort required for identification is not justified, plans have been devised to approximate the cost of the inventory. Several plans of this type, based on the flow of goods, or the flow of costs, are discussed in the following paragraphs.

2. *Average cost.* The *average cost,* or *weighted average cost,* inventory method prices each unit at the average cost of all similar units available for sale during the period. The average unit cost is obtained by dividing the total cost of all units available for sale by the number of the units.

3. *Moving average cost.* A *moving average cost* basis provides an acceptable method for valuing a perpetual inventory. The moving, or running, average is recomputed for a specific item of merchandise on hand after each purchase.

4. *Standard cost.* Manufacturing concerns frequently adopt a predetermined standard cost figure in accounting for the

conversion of raw materials and labor into finished products. *Standard costs*, computed on the basis of past experience and anticipated future conditions, are the costs that, in the opinion of management, should be incurred. Variances between the actual and standard costs reveal whether the operations of individuals or departments have met established standards. An inventory based on standard costs does not indicate the actual cost of the merchandise, but what the cost should be.

5. *First-in, first-out.* A merchant's tendency to dispose of merchandise in the order in which it was received provides a logical basis for the assumption that the goods on hand at any time consist of the latest acquisitions. This assumption, based on the flow of goods, justifies the first-in, first-out, or *fifo*, basis for inventory pricing. There will be exceptions when some of the later units are sold before the earlier ones, but unless the exceptions are material, the most recent costs applied to all of the inventory under the fifo method tends to approximate the results obtained by the specific identification method.

6. *Last-in, first-out.* Last-in, first-out, or *lifo*, procedures assume that the most recently acquired merchandise is sold first and that the remaining inventory consists of the beginning inventory and the earliest purchases handled during the accounting period. This assumption almost never agrees with the physical facts. It refers to the flow of costs and not to the flow of physical goods. Lifo supporters contend that profits are stated more accurately when current costs are applied to merchandise sold, thus permitting replenishment of the stock at approximately the same current prices and achieving a better matching of costs and revenues.

7. *Lower of cost or market.* A popular basis for inventory valuation is *cost or market, whichever is lower.* This method compares actual cost of the inventory items with current market price and uses the lower of the two. Market in this instance means current replacement cost. The cost-or-market plan supports the conservative accounting viewpoint, which holds that profit should not be antici-

pated in the records but provision should be made for all losses. Inventory items, therefore, must not be valued at more than cost, since to do so would make the books show a profit before the sale of the goods. However, any loss due to a decrease in value of merchandise on hand is provided for by listing the items at a figure below cost that represents their present market values or current replacement cost.

8. *Replacement cost.* The *replacement cost* basis for valuing an inventory ignores the actual amount paid for the merchandise on hand and applies instead the current replacement cost of each item. That price would presumably be the cost if the merchandise were purchased at the inventory date in the usual quantities and through the regular channels. The resulting total inventory figure will differ only slightly from the total obtained by the fifo method if the purchase prices are somewhat stable, or if the merchandise has a rapid turnover so that a large proportion of the inventory has been purchased recently. An objection to the replacement cost basis, however, is that those inventory items whose prices have increased will be included at amounts higher than cost, thus showing a profit before sale.

9. *Market price.* An enterprise whose products are traded on a highly organized market sometimes values its inventory at *market* or *selling price.* Examples of such products are cattle, wheat, and gold, whose current market prices are constantly available. This method anticipates profits by pricing the inventory at current selling prices instead of cost.

CHAPTER 9

Sundry Adjustments

ACCRUED AND DEFERRED ITEMS

Interest and Discount. *Interest* is compensation for the use of money. Interest is usually paid at the maturity of a short-term note; on a long-term note or bond, it is paid monthly, quarterly, semiannually, or annually. When interest is collected in advance, it is termed *discount*. Borrowing money from banks often involves discounting a note, which means that the bank collects the interest for the time covered by the note when it makes the loan.

All notes earn interest, in a sense, even if they state that they bear no interest. The present value of any note is its maturity value less its discount to the present time. If a noninterest-bearing note is received from a customer, the interest that is foregone is equivalent to an additional sales discount given to the customer.

On notes receivable, a proportionate share of the interest is earned each day. When using the accrual method, it is necessary to adjust the interest account at the close of each fiscal period to take into consideration any unpaid interest that an obligation has earned during the fiscal period. The interest that has been earned but not yet received is termed *accrued interest receivable,* whereas interest that has been received but not yet earned is termed *interest received in advance.* The interest expense arising from notes payable must also be adjusted at the end of each fiscal period. Interest that has been paid but not yet consumed is a deferred expense, termed *prepaid interest,* whereas interest that has been consumed but not yet paid is termed *accrued interest payable.*

Insurance. Under ordinary circumstances, insurance premiums are paid before the insurance goes into effect, at which time the amount paid is an asset—prepaid insurance. As each day passes, a proportionate share of that premium is consumed and becomes insurance expense. In this instance, however, as in the case of most accrued and deferred items, the amount of the expense is not computed day by day, but adjustment is made at the close of the fiscal period. Then, the asset account is decreased, and the expense account is established for the amount of the expired insurance.

Another method of recording insurance premiums debits the full amount of the premium to insurance expense at the time of payment. At the close of the fiscal period, prepaid insurance is debited and insurance expense is credited for the amount of the unexpired insurance. Both methods achieve the same results when the accounts are adjusted at the close of the fiscal period.

Supplies. At the time of acquisition, supplies are treated either as an asset or as an expense. If treated as an asset, the asset account must be decreased at the close of the fiscal period, when an inventory of supplies is taken, by debiting a supplies used account or a supplies expense account and crediting the supplies account for the amount of supplies consumed. If supplies are recorded as an expense when acquired, an asset account must be set up at the end of the fiscal period for the amount of supplies on hand, and the expense account must be decreased by the same amount.

Other Accrued and Deferred Items. Various other accounts are adjusted at the close of each fiscal period in a manner similar to that indicated above. Some examples are: rent, commissions, wages, and royalties. These may be either income or expense accounts.

Effects on the Accounts. Accrued and deferred items, such as those discussed in the preceding paragraphs, have the following effects on the accounts when the adjustments are recorded:

Adjustment	Dr.	Cr.
Income earned but not previously recorded	Asset (increase)	Income (increase)
Expense accrued but not paid and not previously recorded	Expense (increase)	Liability (increase)
Income received in advance and credited to income when received	Income (decrease)	Liability (increase)
or		
Income received in advance and credited to a liability account when received	Liability (decrease)	Income (increase)
Expense paid in advance and debited to expense when paid	Asset (increase)	Expense (decrease)
or		
Expense paid in advance and debited to an asset account when paid	Expense (increase)	Asset (decrease)

CONTRA ACCOUNTS

A contra account is also known as a *valuation account,* or an *offset account,* and, when related to an asset account, it has a credit balance and is sometimes called a *negative asset account,* a *minus asset account,* or an *asset reduction account.* A *contra account* is defined as an account that relates to, and wholly or partially offsets, one or more other accounts. Thus two accounts can be used to show the present reduced book value of a single item. When this is done, one account discloses the original basis, which in the case of an asset is usually cost, and the other account shows the decrease, which frequently has to be estimated. The resulting net figure is the *balance sheet valuation,* or *book value,* of that item.

The terms *valuation* and *value* must be interpreted with care. For example, the balance sheet valuation of accounts receivable differs from that of a business building. When the accounts receivable total is reduced by the valuation account, allowance for bad debts, the net figure is presumably the estimated amount that will eventually be collected on these accounts. It is the estimated realizable value of the accounts receivable. When a building is listed at cost less accumulated depreciation, the net figure sometimes bears little relationship to the present market value of the building, but is the estimated portion of its original cost that has not yet expired and will be allocated to the costs of future periods. Since the building probably is not being held for sale, its current market value is of less significance, ordinarily, than the undepreciated portion of its cost that is to be recovered through future operations.

Allowance and, to a limited extent, *provision* are terms that have replaced *reserve* extensively in recent years. When used as part of the title of a contra account, they are considered more precise than the term *reserve* and therefore less likely to be misinterpreted by readers of financial statements.

Some contra accounts, such as allowance for bad debts, allowance for depreciation, allowance for depletion, allowance for exhaustion, and unamortized discount on bonds payable, usually require adjustment periodically; but others, including sales returns and allowances, purchase returns and allowances, and discount on capital stock, rarely need an adjustment.

DEPRECIATION AND DEPLETION

Depreciation. A decrease in the value of a fixed asset is called *depreciation* when it is due to the passage of time, wear and tear, obsolescence, or inadequacy. Depreciation may be both physical and nonphysical (or functional). The *physical* factor includes deterioration due to the passage of time and the action of the elements, as well as the wear and tear due to use of the asset. The *nonphysical* factor includes supersession or inadequacy, which is due to the need for replacing an asset with a larger unit, and obsolescence, which is due to inventions or other changes in assets that provide an opportunity to replace present units with more efficient ones.

Depreciation is recorded so that the cost or other basic value of a tangible fixed asset, less salvage value (if any), can be distributed systematically over its estimated useful life. Depreciation is not a process of valuation. The cost of a building less accumulated depreciation does not purport to indicate market value of the building, which fluctuates from time to time, but shows, instead, unallocated cost, or undepreciated cost, to be assigned to later accounting periods.

Methods of Computing Depreciation. Because of the great variety of assets that are used by business enterprises, there must of necessity be a variety of ways of computing the depreciation on such assets so that the depreciation will be as nearly as possible in accord with the facts of each case. Methods of computing depreciation fall principally into two classifications: methods that consider depreciation a function of time and methods that consider depreciation a function of use.

Depreciation as a Function of Time. When depreciation is treated as a function of time, it may be computed by one of the following three methods:

1. *The straight-line method.* With this method, the life of the asset is estimated, and an equal part of the depreciable value of the asset is charged off each accounting period during the life of the asset. The depreciable value is computed by subtracting the estimated scrap value or salvage value from the original cost. The straight-line method is the one most frequently employed because it is the easiest to compute and use, and in many instances, satisfactorily accurate.

2. *An increasing-rate method.* Such a method ordinarily provides a constantly increasing charge for depreciation, and the depreciated value of the asset tends to measure its usefulness. Examples of increasing-rate methods are:

   a. The *sinking-fund method,* which requires equal amounts to be paid into a fund each accounting period. The assets in the fund earn interest that is added to the fund and thus at the end of the useful life of the asset, the total in the fund should equal the depreciable value.

   b. The *increasing-fraction method,* which computes the charge to depreciation as a fractional part of the depreciable value. The life of the asset is estimated in terms of the number of years of useful life. The denominators of all the fractions are the same, that is, the sum of the numbers of years. The numerators of the fractions are the numbers of the years used in sequence beginning with 1 and increasing each year in consecutive order.

3. A *decreasing-rate method*. Such a method provides a constantly decreasing charge for depreciation, and the depreciated value of the asset tends to follow market value. Examples of decreasing-rate methods are:

a. The *declining-balance method,* or *uniform-rate-on-a-diminishing-value method,* which is computed by charging a constant percentage against the depreciated balance, or declining balance, each year. For income tax purposes, the percentage is permitted, with some restrictions, to be twice the percentage that would be allowed with the straight-line method.

b. The *reducing-fraction method,* referred to generally as the *sum-of-the-years'-digits method,* which is computed in a manner similar to that of the increasing-fraction method, discussed above. The difference is that the numerators are the numbers of the fiscal periods used in reverse order.

Depreciation a Function of Use. When depreciation is treated as a function of use, it is computed on the following bases:

1. *Units of production.* This method charges depreciation in accordance with the number of units the particular asset has produced during the fiscal period. The life of the asset is estimated in terms of units of production, and the depreciable value is divided by this number of units to determine how much should be charged to depreciation for each unit of production.

2. *Hours of operation.* This method charges depreciation in accordance with the number of hours the particular asset has been used during the fiscal period. The life of the asset is estimated in terms of hours of use, and the depreciable value is divided by this number of hours to determine how much should be charged to depreciation for each hour of use.

3. *A percentage of sales.* This method computes depreciation

as a fixed percentage of the sales. The charge for depreciation varies in direct relation to the volume of production.

Special Depreciation Methods. Most of the methods of computing depreciation have been discussed in the foregoing classifications and subclassifications. There are other methods, however, that relate to special conditions and assets, such as: the annuity method; the discount method; the appraisal, or revaluation, method; the replacement, or renewal, method; and the insurance, or actuarial, method. Various titles are sometimes given to these methods.

Depreciation Rates. Rates of depreciation are usually established by an enterprise on the basis of its past experience or with the assistance of published material on the subject. *Depreciation Guide Lines and Rules, Revenue Procedure 62-21,* published by the United States Treasury Department Internal Revenue Service, is a valuable aid, as it indicates treasury policy relating to useful lives of business property. Trade association manuals and other business publications can also supply useful information.

In order to be as accurate as possible, depreciation is sometimes computed on each individual asset at an appropriate rate determined by its estimated useful life. This can be done under any of the methods listed above. However, a *composite rate,* or *blanket rate,* for assets of a similar kind, is usually adopted. Use of a composite rate requires less detailed record keeping, since depreciation is computed for a group of assets at a rate that is approximately the average for the group.

Methods of Recording Depreciation. The amount of estimated depreciation of a specific asset or group of assets for a fiscal period is charged to a depreciation expense account and credited to a contra account, such as allowance for depreciation, or accumulated depreciation, for that particular asset or group of assets. The once popular title *reserve for depreciation* is now used infrequently.

In an unusual situation where no contra account is desired, the debit is made to a depreciation expense account, as above, but the credit is entered in the asset account in order to reduce it to the estimated net depreciated value. This method obscures the original cost of the asset.

Depletion. The loss of value that accompanies extractive operations on wasting assets, or exhaustive assets, such as oil wells, mineral deposits, and timberland, is known as *depletion*. It is similar to depreciation, but the terms should be distinguished from each other.

There are several methods of computing depletion. One of the commonest is the production method. Under such a plan, total depletion is obtained by subtracting from the total cost of the asset the estimated value of the land after the natural resources are removed. The number of units of the asset to be removed is estimated, and this number is divided into the total depletion to give the unit depletion cost. Depletion for a fiscal period is then computed by multiplying the number of units removed during that period by the unit depletion cost.

Depletion is usually recorded by debiting an account for depletion expense and crediting a contra account, such as allowance for depletion.

BAD DEBTS

Bad debts, or *uncollectible notes and accounts receivable,* are generally encountered in an enterprise that does business on a credit basis. An uncollectible account is usually found to be uncollectible in an accounting period subsequent to the one in which the sale was made. Sales vary in volume from one accounting period to another, causing variations in the amount of bad debts expense. Each accounting period should bear its expenses, and therefore, in order to allocate bad debts expense acceptably to the accounting periods in which the related sales were made, an adjustment is recorded at the end of each period for the estimated loss from bad debts.

Methods of Computing Bad Debts. On the basis of past experience, there are two principal methods of computing the estimated loss from bad debts. One emphasizes the bad debts expense, computing it as a fixed percentage of accounts receivable, total receivables, net sales, or sales on credit. The other emphasizes the allowance for bad debts, adding to the allowance only enough to make the total a predetermined percentage of the accounts receivable, or of the total receivables, at the close of the fiscal period. Under the second method, the amount of bad debts expense is given secondary consideration, being dependent upon the size of the allowance for bad debts.

Various other methods are used. One is to examine and study the accounts receivable to determine which ones may be uncollectible. Such a study is expedited by *aging* the accounts receivable. Accounts are aged by classifying the unpaid amounts according to date of charge or date due. Another method, not entirely compatible with accrual accounting, is to make no adjustments, but merely to charge off individual accounts to bad debts expense when they are found to be uncollectible. A firm should consider the possible uncollectibility of its notes receivable, loans to employees, and accounts receivable when providing for bad debts.

Methods of Recording Bad Debts. Estimated loss from bad debts for a fiscal period is charged at the close of that period to an expense account, such as bad debts expense, loss from bad debts, loss from doubtful notes and accounts receivable, uncollectible notes and accounts expense, or uncollectible receivables expense. The corresponding credit is made to the allowance for bad debts account, also known as allowance for doubtful receivables, allowance for uncollectible notes and accounts, allowance for credit losses, allowance for collection losses, and provision for doubtful receivables.

When a note is dishonored, or not paid at maturity, or an account receivable proves to be uncollectible, the usual adjusting entry debits the amount to the allowance for bad debts account and credits the asset account.

CHAPTER 10

Division of the Basic Books

NEED FOR SUBDIVISION

All the transactions of a business may be recorded in a simple two-column journal and a ledger containing the ordinary standard form of accounts. However, such a simple plan for the financial records is not efficient if a large volume of business is transacted. Many business enterprises find that they can use subdivisions of these basic books advantageously. They classify their transactions and place the types that occur most frequently in special columns in the general journal or in separate special journals; and when they have a substantial number of accounts they segregate some of them in subsidiary ledgers.

Special journals and special or subsidiary ledgers are used in enterprises of every size and are considered indispensable for large and complex business organizations.

SPECIAL COLUMNS

Columnar General Journal. Any journal with more than one debit column or more than one credit column is a *special-column journal.* Special-column journals bear a variety of other names, such as *columnar journals, divided-column journals, multiple-column journals,* and *multi-column journals.* The introduction of special columns into the general journal provides a simple method for saving time and space in the bookkeeping process. A small enterprise may operate without the help of special journals, but when entries affecting one account occur repeatedly, the work of posting can be reduced materially by placing one or more special columns in the general journal.

A special column relates to one general ledger account only, and contains debits only or credits only. It provides an initial segregation of one type of item. Later, usually at the end of the month, the total of the column is posted as one amount. Thus one posting to the ledger account takes the place of a number of entries, which would have to be made if each amount appearing in the column were posted separately.

Structure of the Columnar General Journal. The number of special columns to be used is a matter of expediency, varying according to the convenience of those who use them. Too many columns will make the journal unwieldy, a condition that may be prevented by the introduction of special journals. Every additional column also increases the number of spaces in which an amount may be placed erroneously.

Special columns are often used for such accounts as cash, accounts receivable, accounts payable, sales, and purchases. If separate special journals are desired for some of the transactions, such as cash receipts and disbursements, the general journal may still contain special columns for other common transactions. Whether or not the general journal contains special columns, it does not give up the two columns for *miscellaneous* debits and credits. These general columns are sometimes called *sundry*, or *general-ledger*, columns. They are needed for entries affecting accounts for which special columns have not been provided. Column headings ordinarily do not appear in a two-column journal, but they are needed to avoid confusion when special columns are used.

In appearance, the columnar general journal may be similar to the two-column journal with added space for the special columns, but there is no standard form.

Entries in the Columnar General Journal. Transactions may be journalized in a columnar general journal with a separate line for each debit and each credit item, as in the two-column form, but space can be saved by using only one line for entries that use the special columns.

The following example shows how an entry can be made on one line to journalize the purchase of an office chair for sixty dollars cash: (1) Place the date in the date column; (2) in the column for account names, write the name of the account to be debited—office equipment—since presumably there is no special column for this account; (3) in the column for explanations, on the same line if there is enough room, write a brief explanation of the transaction, such as "chair from X Co."; (4) in the column for miscellaneous debits, enter the amount, $60.00; and (5) enter the same amount on the same line in the column for cash credits. In this manner, a journal entry is made on one line, whereas in a two-column journal, it would require at least three lines, one each for the debit, the credit, and the explanation. It is not necessary to write the name of the cash account, because the item will later be posted to the credit side of the cash account as part of the total of the column for cash credits.

Combined Cash Journal. Small enterprises, if they have simple bookkeeping requirements, sometimes confine all of their journalizing to a columnar general journal. They may use a simple two-column journal, but the addition of special columns usually promotes efficiency. Cash transactions occur so frequently that, in the absence of separate journals for cash, the columnar general journal is almost certain to have special columns for cash debits and for cash credits. This book is merely a general journal in which to record all transactions, but because of the importance of the cash transactions it is often called the *combined cash journal.* This is the type of book in which the journal entry described above is made. It is practicable only when there are few transactions to record.

Columnar general journals have various titles, such as cash journal, combined cash journal, combination journal, cashbook and journal, or simply, the journal. When there are special cash journals, the general journal does not contain a record of cash transactions, and should not have the term *cash* in its title.

Account Type of Journal. A book that combines the functions of a journal and a ledger is sometimes used in a small business or for personal records. In this *account type of journal,* special columns, using a debit column and a credit column for each account, take the place of a few, or all, of the ledger accounts that would ordinarily appear in a ledger. Balances are carried forward so that the account columns contain all of the information needed in an account, including, at the end of an accounting period, the necessary totals and balances for the financial statements. This form of *journal-ledger, or synoptic journal,* is practicable only when one journal and a few ledger accounts are a sufficient record.

Columnar Special Journals. When special journals are used, they provide an initial segregation of transactions by types according to the kind of journal. This is true whether the journal has one amount column or many. A cash disbursements journal, for instance, will contain a record of transactions involving cash credits. The corresponding debits can be subdivided into classes of entries by using a special column for each important class. Additional columns are often provided for crediting accounts other than cash. An example is purchase discounts.

Columnar Ledger Accounts. A *columnar ledger account* is an analytical type of account that supplies the information given by an ordinary ledger account and, in addition, contains amount columns in which the items making up the account may be distributed by classes. The additional columns provide an analysis of the account.

A ledger account may contain several kinds of information, which are properly combined for the sake of simplicity or some other reason. If it is desirable to segregate this information by classes, a separate general ledger account can be opened for each class, or a controlling account in the general ledger accompanied by subsidiary accounts in a separate ledger can be used. When there are only a few classes of items, columnar ledger accounts offer a third method, providing another application of the controlling account.

A columnar ledger account combines, on one bookkeeping form, the functions of a controlling account and a subsidiary ledger. Two columns ordinarily contain postings for the entire account. They constitute a controlling account for the remaining columns, each of which is the equivalent of an account in a subsidiary ledger.

SPECIAL JOURNALS

A *special journal* is a book of original entry in which specific types of transactions, similar in that they have a like effect on a particular account, are segregated. A special journal is known by such terms as *journal, book, register,* or *record.* It is a laborsaving device designed to increase bookkeeping efficiency. It is especially useful when large numbers of transactions can be segregated into classes so that group totals, instead of individual items, can be posted.

Special journals provide space for a large proportion of the entries that would otherwise have to be made in the general journal, and thus they reduce the bulk of the general journal. They also permit more clerks to work on the books at one time than would be possible if only one journal were used.

Kinds of Special Journals. A few types of transactions occur so frequently that they have brought about the widespread use of four special journals to supplement the general journal, as follows:

1. Cash receipts journal
2. Cash disbursements journal or cash payments journal
3. Purchase journal
4. Sales journal.

All cash transactions are often journalized in one book, known as the *cashbook,* which is a combination of the cash receipts journal and the cash disbursements journal. The cashbook may show the cash receipts and disbursements on opposite pages, the cash receipts being entered on the left-hand page and the cash disbursements on the right-hand page.

Many other journals, such as the voucher register, sales returns and allowances book, notes receivable register, and requisition journal, are useful where the transactions that they record occur in sufficient volume. A register, as explained in the following chapter, usually supplements the information given in the journals and ledgers, but in some instances, also serves as a special journal or a subsidiary ledger.

A private journal is a special journal in which information is recorded that the management considers confidential and desires for some reason to withhold from the accounting department. Such information may deal with matters like salaries or officers' accounts. The private journal is rarely used. When used, it is generally accompanied by a private ledger.

Forms of Special Journals. A wide variation in the number and arrangement of columns in a special journal is possible, depending upon the needs and preferences of those using the books. There may be any number of debit and credit columns, arranged in any order. Date, explanation, and folio columns may also appear in any order. A column heading should make clear the purpose of each column. As in the case of the general journal, a large number of columns will make a special journal unwieldy and will increase the possibility of entering an amount in the wrong column.

Single-Column Special Journals. Perhaps the simplest form of special journal is the single-column form. This type of journal has only one money column. The first column ordinarily contains the date; the second shows for each transaction the name of the account not provided for by an amount column; the third is used for necessary details explaining the transaction; the fourth is the ledger folio column; and the fifth is the money, or amount, column.

This form can be used only when all of the transactions it records affect one account in the same manner, either to debit it or to credit it. A sales book, for example, may be a single-column journal. Only sales will be journalized in it. Periodically, probably at the end of each month, the one money column is totaled and the amount posted to the credit side of the sales account. Debit items are posted individually to their several accounts, and the sum of all the separate debit postings from the sales journal should equal the one credit to the sales account.

If controlling accounts are used and all sales are made to customers on account, only two postings are periodically required to the general ledger from the single-column sales book. The total of the amount column is debited to the accounts receivable controlling account and credited to the sales account.

A variation of this method, sometimes employed, but without the need of a separate sales journal, involves: filing an extra copy of each sales invoice in a special file or binder, either in numerical or date order; running an adding machine tape of the invoices at the end of each month; and debiting the total to the accounts receivable controlling account and crediting it to the sales account. The file of invoices and the accompanying tape thus take the place of a sales journal. When the invoices are numbered, their continuity can be readily ascertained to insure that all invoices are accounted for.

There are relatively few situations in which single-column journals are satisfactory; hence, most journals have two or more columns.

Multiple-Column Special Journals. Transactions occurring frequently enough to justify the use of special journals usually require further analysis so that business management may have the detailed financial information it needs. Such additional analysis is possible in multiple-column special journals, where special columns similar to those found in a columnar general journal provide for the subclassification of similar types of items. For instance, the management may desire an analysis of sales by commodities or by departments of the business. Special columns in a multiple-column sales book can supply such information. Cash payments always create a credit to the cash account, but they also require an occasional credit to the purchase discounts account, as well as debits to the accounts payable account and to a variety of expense accounts. Special columns in the cash disbursements book provide a medium for the segregation of these various elements.

Advantages of Special Journals. Some of the advantages of special journals are the following:

1. They segregate types of transactions and keep them from being scattered throughout the general journal, thus reducing the bulk of the general journal and simplifying the reference to a particular transaction or to the type as a whole.

2. They save labor, as the grouping of similar transactions and the increased use of special columns minimizes the need for writing account names and explanations in journalizing, and the columnar totals reduce the amount of posting and relieve the ledger of a mass of details.

3. They facilitate the use of controlling accounts and subsidiary ledgers by supplying the necessary totals and details.

4. They reduce errors because of simplified entries and simplified posting.

5. They enable more than one bookkeeper to work on the books at the same time when there is too much work for one person.

6. They facilitate division of labor, distributing the work among the bookkeepers so that each may become proficient by specializing in a few tasks. No time is lost in shifting from one operation to another, and individuals with limited bookkeeping knowledge can readily be trained to handle many of the operations.

7. They help make effective a system of internal check, or internal control, in which one employee must check the work of another, thus localizing errors and fixing responsibility.

Disadvantages of Special Journals. With an increase in the number of books used, more space for storage is required, and there is greater danger of misplacing books. A small concern can overcome these disadvantages to some extent by keeping special journals on loose-leaf forms in the same cover with the general journal, using index tabs to separate them.

General Journal Not Supplanted. Even when special journals are employed to the fullest practicable extent, they do not supplant the general journal. This journal continues to be useful for some types of entries that occur too infrequently to warrant setting up special journals. The general journal should contain such entries as: (1) opening entries, (2) entries for unusual transactions, (3) compound entries that cannot readily be shown in their entirety in a special journal, (4) correcting entries, and (5) adjusting, closing, and post-closing entries.

SPECIAL LEDGERS

Subdivision of the General Ledger. As business units grow in size and complexity, they need more accounts to give them adequate financial records. When the accounts become too numerous to be handled conveniently in one general ledger, it is customary to place some of them in special ledgers. When a group of similar accounts is large enough to justify its segregation in a subsidiary ledger, it is often advantageous to remove the group from the general ledger and substitute a controlling account in its place. Conversely, when a single general ledger account proves to be inadequate, a group of related detailed accounts can be established to take its place. Instead of placing all of these new accounts in the general ledger, however, one can place them in a subsidiary ledger, retaining the original general ledger account as a controlling account. There is no definite number of accounts needed to justify a separate subsidiary ledger.

Subsidiary Ledgers. A subsidiary ledger is a ledger that contains a group of related accounts summarized and represented by a controlling account.

Many businesses maintain at least two subsidiary ledgers in addition to the general ledger: one for accounts with customers, which is variously labeled the accounts receivable, sales, or customers' ledger; and one for creditors' accounts, called the accounts payable, purchase, or creditors' ledger. There may be any number of additional subsidiary ledgers, such as expense, capital stock, factory, plant, and private ledgers.

Accounts in a subsidiary ledger are arranged in whatever order is most convenient. They may be written on ordinary standard account forms like those in the general ledger or on a special form planned for a special type of account. Some enterprises prepare an extra file copy of each invoice representing a charge to a customer's account; this copy is inserted in the subsidiary accounts receivable ledger until payment is received and is then removed to a transfer file. This plan provides a customers' ledger, in which the accounts consist of duplicate copies of unpaid invoices. A similar plan can be followed for an accounts payable ledger, in which the accounts consist of a file of unpaid invoices received from creditors.

CONTROLLING ACCOUNTS

A *controlling account* is an account that contains in summary form the information given in detail by a group of related accounts in a subsidiary ledger. In this way, the general ledger can be relieved of many details, which are available in subsidiary ledgers. Conversely, if a general ledger account needs further analysis, subsidiary accounts can be set up to furnish the necessary details.

The close relationship between these accounts requires that every item in a subsidiary account must be represented in the controlling account. Every journal entry that affects any subsidiary account must have the same effect on its controlling account, either as a separate posting or as part of a total. At the end of an accounting period, the balance in a controlling account must equal the combined balances of the subsidiary accounts that it controls.

Extent of Use of Controlling Accounts. In a small business, accounts receivable and accounts payable are often the only controlling accounts needed, but in a large concern, most of the general ledger accounts may be controlling accounts. Any general ledger account can be made a controlling account simply by establishing a group of subsidiary accounts in which the information contained in the general ledger account is amplified to any extent desired.

Sometimes, if the information desired in support of a controlling account cannot be disclosed adequately with one series of subsidiary accounts, additional series of subsidiary accounts may be required. This makes each of the first series of subsidiary accounts an intermediate controlling account, summarizing its section of the second series, and all of the intermediate controlling accounts in the series are summarized in turn in one controlling account in the general ledger. As need arises, one or more accounts in the second series may be subdivided further in the same manner.

Titles and Forms of Controlling Accounts. An account may have a distinctive title to indicate that it is a controlling account, but it does not need one. For instance, the general ledger controlling account for customers' accounts is often called simply *accounts receivable*. Other names given the accounts receivable controlling account are *accounts receivable—control, accounts receivable—trade, customers' accounts,* or *trade debtors*. The controlling account for accounts payable is given such titles as *accounts payable, accounts payable—control, accounts payable—trade, creditors' accounts,* and *trade creditors*.

The same form of ruling that is used for other general ledger accounts is usually employed for controlling accounts. If there are but a few subsidiary accounts, a columnar form of ledger account may be desirable.

SELF-BALANCING SPECIAL LEDGERS

A subsidiary ledger ordinarily contains an excess of debits, or of credits, equal in amount to the balance in the controlling account. Such a ledger can be converted into a self-balancing ledger by the simple expedient of inserting in it a memorandum account and posting totals to it that are just the opposite of all entries posted to the individual accounts.

This balancing account then contains the same kind of summary information that is posted to the controlling account in the general ledger, but the amounts are on the opposite side of the account. The balances of the two accounts must be the same amount, but one will be a debit and the other a credit. The controlling account and the subsidiary ledger balancing account are often referred to as reciprocal accounts or *interlocking accounts*. The memorandum balancing account in a subsidiary ledger has a variety of names, such as *general ledger, home office, main office, balancing account, general balancing account,* and *general ledger adjustment*.

A subsidiary ledger, such as a factory ledger or a branch ledger, which is kept at some distance from the general ledger, may contain a balancing account to assist the bookkeeper in determining readily whether or not his ledger is in balance. Frequently, however, there is no particular advantage in maintaining the self-balancing feature when the ledgers are in the same office, for then the accuracy of the subsidiary ledger totals is readily tested by making an abstract or schedule of them for comparison with the controlling account.

ADVANTAGES OF SUBSIDIARY LEDGERS AND CONTROLLING ACCOUNTS

Subsidiary ledgers, controlling accounts, and special journals have somewhat similar advantages, because they supplement each other. The principal advantages of special journals are listed on pages 90 and 91. Advantages of subsidiary ledgers and controlling accounts are as follows:

1. They segregate types of accounts and thus provide a logical grouping of similar items.
2. They keep down the bulk of the general ledger by substituting a controlling account for a group of accounts, thus shortening the trial balance and simplifying the preparation of financial statements.
3. They provide details and summaries; the subsidiary ledgers contain the individual items that the controlling accounts represent with totals.
4. They reduce errors.
5. They enable more than one bookkeeper to work on the books at the same time.
6. They facilitate division of labor.
7. They help make a system of internal control effective.

Since the last four advantages listed above are identical with the last four advantages of special journals, previously listed, they are not explained here.

PROCEDURES WITH SPECIAL JOURNALS AND SPECIAL LEDGERS

Entries in Columnar Journals. Procedures for recording transactions in special-column journals are indicated in general terms as follows:

1. Place the date of each transaction in the date column.

Some bookkeepers prefer to show the date in the middle of the page just before each entry. Others place it at the top of the page and do not repeat it unless the date changes. When the date column is used, it is desirable to show the year at the top of the column, and the month and day on the line on which the first entry begins. Subsequent entries may include the month and day, the day only, or no date if it is the same as the preceding entry.

2. In the column for account names, place the name of any general ledger account to be debited if there is no special column for this account. If there are several such debits, use a separate line for each.

3. Place the amount for each of the foregoing accounts in the column for miscellaneous debits on the line bearing the name of the account to be debited.

4. On the next line, directly beneath the last name in the account-names column, write the name of any general ledger account to be credited, if there is no special column for this account.

5. Write the amount of the credit for the foregoing account on the same line in the column for miscellaneous credits.

6. If either a debit or a credit item belongs in a special column, place it there; and in the column for account names, give the name of the subsidiary account involved, if any. It is not necessary to write the name of the general ledger account affected, since this name appears at the head of the special column in which the item is entered. To save space, items in special columns can be placed on the same line with other items, except when a separate line is necessary for proper identification in the account-names column.

7. Write a brief explanation in the column for explanations, unless the transaction was so simple and so common that no further details will be needed in the future to support this entry. Sometimes there is only one column for account names and explanations. Then the explanation may be written across the entire column, beginning on the line following the first part of the entry, as in the two-column general journal. In order to save space, it may be written at

the right side of the account name, in the same column and on the same line.

8. Ordinarily, do not write anything in the folio column until the items are posted to the ledger accounts.

The instructions given above (except number 6) apply to transactions recorded in the miscellaneous, or sundry, columns. In the special columns, entries record transactions that are relatively simple and occur frequently; consequently they require a minimum of explanation and usually only one line each in the journal.

The general journal always requires two sundry columns, one for debits and one for credits, so that any kind of transaction can be recorded in it. A special journal limits the kinds of transactions it records and thus, ordinarily, needs only one sundry column, or none at all.

Proving the Journal. In order to be sure that the debits and credits in a journal are equal, the journal should be *proved* by footing the amount columns and seeing that the sum of the debit-column totals agrees with the sum of the credit-column totals. It is not necessary to write the totals in a two-column general column, where each item is posted separately. When more columns are used, however, most of them require totals for posting purposes, and it is customary to show the totals for all of them as an aid in proving the journal.

Many bookkeepers prefer to write the totals at the bottom of each page and to carry them forward to the proper columns at the top of the next page so that the equality of the debits and credits can be tested on each page when it is completed, instead of waiting until the end of the accounting period.

Posting to Subsidiary Ledgers. When subsidiary accounts are used, it is customary to have special columns in the journals in which to record transactions affecting such accounts, in order to provide not only the details for the subsidiary accounts, but totals, as well, for the controlling accounts. The details are posted to the subsidiary accounts when convenient, perhaps daily, in order to keep the accounts up to date. The column totals are posted to the controlling accounts only at monthly or other infrequent intervals.

When posting to subsidiary accounts from a special column in a journal, the bookkeeper obtains the amount from the special column and the name of the account from the column for account names. He enters in the account the date of the transaction, the journal page on which it is recorded, the amount, and if necessary, a very brief description. He places the ledger page number, or the account number, in the folio column in the journal on the line containing the item posted. If neither the ledger pages nor the accounts are numbered, a check mark placed in the folio column in the journal indicates a completed posting. Some bookkeepers prefer to place the account numbers in the journal when journalizing so that the accounts can be found more readily when posting. In that event, after an item has been posted, a check mark is placed in the journal beside the account number or beside the amount.

It is possible at times to improve the bookkeeping procedures by journalizing groups of transactions in summary form instead of making a separate journal entry for each individual transaction. For example, the duplicate copies of invoices representing sales to customers on account may be totaled and recorded periodically, perhaps daily or monthly, so that one journal entry covers many sales. This procedure was touched upon earlier in this chapter in the discussion of single-column special journals. Under this plan, posting to the individual subsidiary accounts with customers is made directly from the duplicate invoices, unless the customers' ledger consists of copies of unpaid invoices, as mentioned in the section on subsidiary ledgers. In either case, the customers' accounts can be kept up to date continuously, whereas the total sales of the month will be posted from the journal to the general ledger at the end of the month.

Sometimes, an item affecting a subsidiary account appears in the sundry debits column or the sundry credits column of a journal, because there is no special column for it. Such an item will be posted to the subsidiary account in the same manner as if it were journalized in a special column. It will also be posted to the controlling account as an individual item, and special care must be exercised in order to be sure that both postings are made.

Posting from Columnar Journals to the General Ledger. Ordinarily, a special-column journal has a column for sundry debits or one for sundry credits or one for each, containing items for which no special columns are provided. Such items are posted individually to the general ledger accounts in a manner similar to that employed in posting to a subsidiary account. Totals of the sundry columns are never posted, since the items comprising them are posted individually.

Special columns, on the other hand, are posted to the general ledger accounts by totals, never by items. The heading of a special column contains the name of the general ledger account to which the total is to be posted and indicates whether the items in the column are debits or credits. The date of the entry in the ledger is the date on which the special column was totaled, usually the last day of the month. A notation at the foot of the column, perhaps enclosed in a circle just below the total, indicates that the total has been posted.

It is important to indicate by a notation in the journal, such as a ledger page number, an account number, or a check mark, that an individual item or a column total has been posted. Thus a glance at a journal page can reveal whether or not all of the items have been posted.

General Ledger in Balance Periodically. Items that appear in the sundry columns of the journals are posted to the general ledger day by day at any convenient time, whereas special columns are totaled and posted only at the close of the month or at other periodic intervals. The general ledger, therefore, does not balance throughout the period, but only after all of the postings have been made at the end of the period.

Comparison of Subsidiary Ledgers and Controlling Account Balances. Periodically, a comparison should be made between the balance of a controlling account and the sum of the balances of the subsidiary accounts that it controls. This is accomplished by listing the subsidiary account balances, the total of which should agree with the balance of the controlling account. When such a list includes the names of the subsidiary accounts, with their balances, it is called a list, an abstract, or a schedule of these accounts.

Transactions Involving Several Journals. Sometimes it is desirable to record part, or all, of a transaction in more than one journal in order to utilize special columns. For instance, the bookkeeper may record a cash sale in both the cash receipts book and the sales book. In the cash receipts book, he enters the amount of the transaction in the special column for cash debits and also in the column for sundry credits, indicating in the column for account names that the sundry credit is a sales account item. At the same time, he enters the transaction in the sales book, crediting the sales account in the special column for sales and debiting the cash account in the sundry debits column. He then places a check mark in both journals in the folio columns to indicate that the sundry items are not to be posted. Thus there will be only one cash debit for the transaction, and it will reach the ledger as part of the total of the special column for cash debits in the cash receipts book. There will be only one sales credit, which will be part of the total of the sales column in the sales book.

This method of preventing double posting, by checking duplicate entries in the journals, is known as *blank checking* or *cross checking*.

CHAPTER 11

Auxiliary Records

THE USE OF AUXILIARY RECORDS

Auxiliary records are the records that are maintained by an enterprise in addition to the journals and ledgers. They are supplementary records. They provide management with additional detailed information that cannot be given conveniently or economically in the basic journals and ledgers.

The designation is merely one of convenience, as the distinction between auxiliary records and the basic books is not a fundamental one. Their fields often overlap. Sometimes an auxiliary record takes the place of a special journal or performs the function of a subsidiary ledger. Many kinds of auxiliary records are used. The types found most frequently can be classified as registers and sundry business papers.

REGISTERS

A *register* is a type of record that usually supplements the information given in the journals and ledgers, but, in some instances, also serves as a special journal or a subsidiary ledger. Its form varies according to the purpose for which it is maintained. Frequently it is a columnar form.

Registers for notes receivable, notes payable, and insurance policies are examples of auxiliary records that supplement the information contained in the journals and ledgers. Such registers may provide the details necessary to journalize the transactions and additional information desired by management. The notes receivable and notes payable registers show the data required for the journal and such additional information as due date, date of payment, and interest rate. The insurance policy register provides such information as date of policy, policy number, name of insurance company, property insured, amount of policy, amount of unexpired premium both at the beginning and at the close of the fiscal year, and the amount of the expired premium at the close of the year.

A register is often employed in connection with business papers that are numbered serially. It provides a summarized record of the information contained in the papers and also a control over the papers used, since every one must be accounted for, even though some may be voided or canceled because of errors.

A register may be a book of original entry from which postings are made. It is then a special journal. Examples of this kind of register are the sales register, the check register, and the voucher register. The papers recorded in each of these customarily bear serial numbers. The sales register takes the place of the sales journal, the check register takes the place of the cash disbursements journal, and the voucher register takes the place of the purchase journal.

In some instances, registers serve as subsidiary ledgers. For example, a fixed assets register can supply all of the details needed in support of controlling accounts for machinery and for allowance for depreciation of machinery when it is kept in such a manner that it shows the date of acquisition and cost of each machine, with name of maker and serial number, estimated useful life, estimated final trade-in or scrap value, depreciation computed in previous years, and the monthly charges for depreciation during the current fiscal year.

BUSINESS PAPERS

Business papers, sometimes called *vouchers, supporting documents,* or *underlying documents,* consist of any written matter in addition to the journals and ledgers that may be used as evidence of a business transaction. They assist the accounting department in proving the accuracy of its records. At the time a transaction takes place, some written record is usually made, which lessens the danger of errors and of future misunderstandings between the parties involved.

Business papers are important for the following reasons:

1. They constitute the original data upon which many of the book entries are based.
2. They aid the system of internal control.
3. They are useful for reference and verification.
4. They form a basis for income tax reports, social security and payroll tax reports, and other government reports.
5. They may be a factor in settling legal controversies, as they are sometimes considered more important as evidence than the journals and ledgers, which have been prepared from them.

CLASSIFICATION OF BUSINESS PAPERS

Following is a classified list of some of the more important business papers, described briefly.

Papers Relating to Purchases:

1. *Purchase requisition,* initiating a purchase by indicating the need for commodities
2. *Purchase order,* requesting the vendor to ship goods
3. *Purchase invoice,* prepared by the vendor for the purchaser, usually showing a list of goods shipped, together with prices and terms
4. *Credit memorandum,* issued by the vendor, reducing the amount owed by the purchaser
5. *Voucher,* authorizing entry in the voucher register to record purchase of commodities or services, and at the proper time, authorizing payment by check.

Papers Relating to Sales:

1. *Sales ticket* or *sales slip* or *cash register tape,* giving detailed information concerning a sale
2. *Sales invoice,* prepared by the vendor, giving details of a sale of goods
3. *Credit memorandum,* prepared by the vendor, reducing the amount owed to him

4. *Bill of lading,* relating to a freight shipment
5. *Statement of account,* indicating the status of the account with the customer and sometimes aiding in the collection of the amount due.

Papers Relating to Cash Receipts:

1. *Cash sales ticket,* giving the details of a cash sale
2. *Cash register tape,* listing briefly the cash transactions
3. *Receipt,* issued to the payer, acknowledging cash received
4. *Correspondence,* concerning cash received by the enterprise.

Papers Relating to Cash Disbursements:

1. *Check,* used for making payment, together with the carbon copy or *check stub*
2. *Remittance advice,* describing the purpose of the payment
3. *Voucher,* authorizing payment by check
4. *Petty cash voucher,* explaining small payment in cash, described later in this chapter
5. *Receipt,* for cash paid out.

Papers Relating to Bank Transactions:

1. *Signature card,* furnishing the bank with the signature that the depositor will use in signing checks
2. *Deposit ticket,* or *deposit slip,* a form accompanying a bank deposit and listing the items deposited
3. *Passbook,* a small book in which the bank enters the amount of each deposit as a receipt for the depositor
4. *Checkbook,* a book of detachable blank checks, which provides the depositor with convenient forms for making withdrawals and making payments to others, and check stubs or a check register in which a record of the account may be kept
5. *Debit memorandum* and *credit memorandum,* prepared by the bank to adjust the bank account
6. *Bank statement,* usually a periodic statement for the depositor, showing the deposits, withdrawals, and balance of his account
7. *Bank reconciliation,* described later in the chapter, prepared and used by the depositor to compare the bank statement with his record of the account.

Negotiable Instruments:
1. *Draft* or *commercial draft,* a *bill of exchange,* signed by the drawer, requesting the drawee (usually a debtor) to pay a specified amount of money to a third party, the payee (usually a bank), and frequently specifying that it is payable on sight (a sight draft) or on demand
2. *Trade acceptance* or *time draft,* drawn by one party, requesting another party (the drawee) to pay a specified amount at some later date, say sixty days after the date of the draft, and signed on the face of the draft by the drawee to signify that he accepts the terms of the draft and will pay it at maturity, as if it were a promissory note
3. *Bank check,* drawn on a bank by a depositor
4. *Certified check,* a bank check signed by a depositor and also signed by a representative of the bank certifying that the check is good for the amount specified
5. *Bank draft,* a check drawn by a bank on another bank
6. *Cashier's check,* drawn by a bank on itself
7. *Express money order,* payable at an express company office
8. *Postal money order,* payable at a post office
9. *Promissory note,* an unconditional written promise, made by one person to another, signed by the maker, to pay on demand or at a fixed or determinable future time, to order or to bearer, a certain sum of money
10. *Bond,* as defined in Chapter 15, negotiable if not registered
11. *Warehouse receipt,* showing that goods purchased have been stored, title to which may be transferred by transferring the receipt
12. *Bill of lading,* a written contract in which the carrier acknowledges receipt of goods and agrees to transport them.

Miscellaneous Business Papers:
1. *Ordinary correspondence, contracts, insurance policies, deeds, licenses, inventory sheets, expense bills, mortgages, receipts, statistical reports, letters of credit,* etc.
2. *Journal voucher,* an office form required in some enterprises as the authority for each journal entry.

BANK RECONCILIATION

A business enterprise that maintains one or more bank accounts ordinarily prepares a *bank reconciliation* at the close of each month. An individual should also do this if he has a personal checking account. This is done in order to make a comparison between the bank statement and the depositor's records, and to account for any differences between them. Either the bank or the depositor may have made an error. If the error has been made by the depositor, he should locate it and correct his records. If the error has been made by the bank, the bank should be notified so that proper corrections can be made.

The reconciliation is made by checking the canceled checks returned by the bank against the withdrawals shown on the bank statement and against the cash disbursements book, or perhaps against the check stubs, and checking the deposits listed on the bank statement against the duplicate deposit slips on hand or against the cash receipts book. This procedure permits ready identification of checks drawn but not yet paid and deposits sent to the bank but not yet credited to the account at the reconciliation date. A memorandum record of the reconciliation should be made in the following manner: total the amounts of the outstanding checks, subtract this sum from the balance shown by the bank statement, and add the amounts deposited for which credit has not yet been given. If there are other differences, they should be noted. The resulting figure should be the same as the balance shown by the check stubs and the cash account.

PETTY CASH

There is general agreement that a strict accounting for cash transactions can be obtained more readily if all cash received is deposited in a bank and all disbursements are made by check. Nevertheless, numerous small expenditures must be made from time to time in the average business office for such items as postage stamps, express charges, and messenger service. These expenditures can be made more conveniently with cash than with checks.

The imprest system for handling a *petty cash fund* provides a plan for making minor payments with cash and later repaying the amounts to the fund by check, so that the books will show checks issued for all disbursements. Petty cash expenditures are recorded in the ledger accounts only at intervals, when replenishing checks are issued to cover them.

A petty cash fund is established by drawing and cashing a check, and debiting petty cash and crediting cash with the amount. This cash is kept in a petty cash box, or drawer, separate from incoming cash, and a record of payments from it is maintained in a petty cash book. When a payment is made, the cashier must obtain a receipt for it. Such a receipt, which is necessary to support the petty cash records, is usually called a *petty cash voucher*. The petty cash fund is replenished periodically, or when the cash remaining on hand reaches a predetermined minimum. To replenish the fund, a check is issued for the amount necessary to bring the cash up to the original figure, and petty cash vouchers for that amount are filed as underlying documents supporting the expenditures.

The amount of a replenishing check is debited to the accounts affected, as shown by the petty cash book, and the cash account is credited without affecting the petty cash account, according to one method of accounting for petty cash expenditures. No entries are made in the petty cash account under this method, except when a change in policy requires an increase or decrease in the petty cash fund. The amount of this fund remains constant and must at all times be equal to the total petty cash and petty cash vouchers on hand.

Under another method of accounting for petty cash expenditures, the amount of the check replenishing the fund is debited to the petty cash account and credited to cash. At the same time, the petty cash account is credited with the same amount, and the individual accounts affected by the petty cash payments, as shown by the petty cash book, are debited. Thus the petty cash account reflects the total amounts paid out of the fund and the dates on which replenishing checks were issued, but the amount of the fund does not change.

CHAPTER 12

The Voucher System

A *voucher system* is the part of the accounting system of many enterprises that provides for the verification and prompt recording of all transactions involving cash expenditures and the authorization for such expenditures. Petty cash payments are an apparent exception to this procedure, but when a check is issued to replenish the petty cash fund, it must pass through the same routine as other checks, including verification and approval of the items covered and authorization for issuance of the check.

In some enterprises, the voucher system is not required to include all transactions that involve expenditures. For example, a check may be drawn for an occasional disbursement, such as the payment of a note payable or the purchase of an asset, without a voucher to authorize it. Such departures from a rigid adherence to the voucher system render its control less effective.

Part of the value of the voucher system lies in the fact that it is one of the most important factors in an efficient method of internal control, especially as it relates to the control of expenditures.

THE VOUCHER

As used in the voucher system, a *voucher* is a paper on which a transaction involving an expenditure is summarized and signatures or other marks have been placed that attest to its correctness, authorize its entry in the books, and approve its payment at the proper time. Any business paper may be called a voucher, as indicated in the preceding chapter; therefore, some writers prefer a distinctive title for the vouchers used in the voucher system, such as *accounts payable voucher, formal voucher,* or *cash voucher.* Under the voucher system, no check should be issued unless it is authorized by a voucher.

Form of the Voucher. Vouchers vary considerably in form and in the information they carry, but they have common characteristics. Printed forms are generally used, providing space on one or both sides for such data as the following: name and address of creditor, date of purchase, terms, date that payment is due if discount is taken, final date that entire amount is due, brief description of the transaction, accounts and amounts to be debited and credited, signatures or initials required to provide the necessary authorization, and date of payment and check number. Customarily, an invoice covered by a voucher will be attached to the voucher as a supporting document.

A single copy of a voucher is sufficient in some offices. In others the voucher is prepared with one or more carbon copies to be filed so as to facilitate cross reference. For instance, the original may be filed numerically according to the voucher number, one copy alphabetically according to the vendor's name, and another copy according to the payment date.

The Voucher Check. A *voucher check* is a form of voucher and check combined. It contains information, either on the check itself or on a detachable slip, indicating to the payee the purpose for which the check was issued. The check and the voucher are prepared at the same time, but usually the check is not dated, signed, or numbered until authority is given to send it to the payee. The voucher is merely a carbon copy of the check and accompanying information, to be retained for the office files. Additional details, such as journalizing instructions and approval signatures, may be added to this copy.

Preparation of a Voucher. Vouchers should be prepared promptly in order to keep the records up to date. Necessary documents relating to the transaction to be recorded are attached to the voucher. As the voucher is sent from department to department, each person charged with a responsibility regarding it will make necessary notations on it, initial it, and send it on to the next department. Thus the voucher, with the various notations made on it and the supporting documents attached to it, makes all the necessary information relative to a particular transaction available in one place and fixes a definite responsibility on each person who has made notations on the voucher.

THE VOUCHER REGISTER

A *voucher register* is a special journal in which the vouchers are entered and also a subsidiary ledger showing the unpaid amounts owing to creditors.

The Voucher Register a Journal. A voucher register is an expanded form of purchase journal. The voucher register records transactions that relate to purchases of merchandise for resale, as does the purchase journal, but it also includes all other transactions that involve the disbursement of cash. When a voucher register is used, the check register becomes a simple record, since all checks are recorded with debits to one account only, the vouchers payable account, and credits to cash and occasionally to purchase discounts.

Form of the Voucher Register. Voucher registers, as well as vouchers, vary considerably in form. Like the voucher, the voucher register is designed to meet the requirements of the particular business in which it is used. The voucher register is frequently set up to provide separate columns for each of the following: date of voucher, name of creditor, explanation and terms, voucher number, date of payment, and check number. The voucher register also has an amount column for credits to vouchers payable (or audited vouchers payable or accounts payable), and debit columns that are needed to classify and distribute the expenditures, including an amount column for debits to sundry accounts for which no special columns are provided, and a column for the names of such accounts.

Recording a Voucher. After a voucher has been prepared and its entry properly authorized, it is recorded in the voucher register in its numerical order. It is then placed in the unpaid vouchers file, unless it is to be paid at once. When authorization is given for the payment of a newly made voucher or an older one that is in the unpaid file, a check is drawn according to the information on the voucher. If a voucher check is used, the previously written check is dated, numbered, and signed. The check is entered in the check register; the date and number are placed in the voucher register on the line recording the voucher to indicate its payment; and the voucher is removed to the paid vouchers file.

Posting from the Voucher Register. Items in the voucher register are posted to the general ledger periodically, usually monthly, except sundry debits, which can be posted at anytime. All columns are totaled, as in any columnar journal, and the equality of total debits and total credits is proved. Then the total of each special column is posted to the account indicated in the column heading, and any unposted items in the column for sundry debits are posted individually to the accounts designated in the column for account names.

The Voucher Register a Ledger. The voucher register supplants the accounts payable ledger and thus possesses the attributes of a subsidiary ledger in addition to the previously mentioned journal characteristics. A separate creditors' ledger may be maintained as part of a voucher system, if desired, but the voucher register makes this unnecessary by showing at all times the unpaid amounts still owing to creditors. Such amounts appear in the voucher register as a record of the individual vouchers, arranged in their numerical order, and there may be several amounts owing to the same creditor on different transactions. On the other hand, the accounts in the creditors' ledger, arranged in alphabetical or other desired sequence, give a cumulative history of the transactions with each creditor. Extra effort and expense are required to keep a creditors' ledger, however, and the voucher register is considered to be an ample record by many enterprises, especially if bills are promptly paid so that a list of the unpaid vouchers can readily be prepared.

Abstract of Vouchers Payable. The voucher register provides a ready reference to the vouchers themselves and maintains a control over the file of unpaid vouchers, since the total amount of vouchers listed in the voucher register for which no payment date or check number is shown should agree with the total amount of the vouchers in the unpaid vouchers file.

Periodically, usually at the end of each month, an abstract of vouchers payable is prepared by listing the unpaid vouchers as shown in the voucher register. This list, or schedule, should agree with the vouchers in the unpaid vouchers file. An alternative procedure for the preparation of the abstract is to list the vouchers in the unpaid vouchers file and compare the list with the unpaid vouchers according to the voucher register. The total of the abstract must agree with the balance in the vouchers payable account in the general ledger.

CHAPTER 13

Single Proprietorship and Partnership

As noted in Chapter 1, there are three principal types of business organization in the United States. They are the *single proprietorship*, the *partnership*, and the *corporation*. These organizations differ in structure and in legal technicalities affecting their formation and subsequent actions. Each type has similar accounting requirements relating to the assets and liabilities but uses distinctive *proprietary accounts*. This chapter discusses the single proprietorship and the partnership. The following chapter discusses the corporation.

SINGLE PROPRIETORSHIP

The simplest form of business organization is the *single proprietorship*, sometimes called *sole proprietorship* or *individual proprietorship*. In this type of organization, a single proprietor owns the business and is responsible for its operation. The proprietor is entitled to the profits that are made and must bear the losses, if they occur.

Advantages of the Single Proprietorship. The principal advantages enjoyed by the single proprietorship over other forms of business organization are:

1. Ease of formation—less formality and fewer legal restrictions than for the establishment of other forms
2. Sole ownership of profits—proprietor not required to share profits with anyone
3. Control vested in one owner—no co-owners to consult

4. Flexibility—no permission necessary from the state for performance of any legal act
5. Relative freedom from government control and special taxation.

Disadvantages of the Single Proprietorship.

1. Unlimited liability—individual proprietor responsible for full amount of debts of his business, even though they may exceed his investment
2. Unstable life—enterprise automatically terminated upon death of owner or his disposal of the business
3. Less capital available, ordinarily, than in other types of business organization
4. Difficulty of obtaining long-term loans
5. Narrow viewpoint and limited experience more probable with one owner than with several.

PROPRIETARY ACCOUNTS

In a single proprietorship, two *proprietary accounts* ordinarily record the owner's equity. One is his *capital* account and the other his *personal,* or *drawing,* or *current,* account. Customarily, the personal account is a temporary account and is closed into the capital account at the end of the year.

The capital account is credited with the amount of the original investment, subsequent additional investments, a credit balance transferred from the personal account, and adjustments, if needed. It is debited with the amount of any permanent withdrawal of investment, a debit balance transferred from the personal account, and adjustments, if needed. Unless the liabilities of the enterprise exceed the assets, the capital account should have a credit balance showing the amount of investment.

The personal account is credited with more or less temporary additional investments of money, merchandise, and other assets and with a credit balance transferred from the income summary account. It is debited with withdrawals of money, merchandise, or other assets that occur in relatively small amounts and are considered to be in anticipation of profits (as contrasted with withdrawals of investment), and with a debit balance from the income summary account.

DISPOSITION OF PROFIT AND LOSS

A sole proprietor may withdraw his profits as he sees fit. Generally, he takes them in the form of cash or merchandise, debiting the amounts to his personal account.

The income summary account, which indicates a profit if it has a credit balance and a loss if it has a debit balance, is usually closed to the personal account, as indicated above. In some enterprises, the balance of the income summary account is closed to the proprietors' capital account.

PARTNERSHIP

The Uniform Partnership Act, adopted by various states, defines a *partnership* as "an association of two or more persons to carry on as co-owners a business for profit." A contractual relationship exists among the partners. Some of the characteristics that distinguish a partnership from other forms of business organization are: limited life, unlimited liability of at least one partner, co-ownership of assets, mutual agency, share in management, and share in partnership profits.

Advantages of the Partnership.
1. Ease of formation—few legal formalities compared with requirements for creation of a corporation
2. Direct rewards—partners motivated by direct sharing of profits to apply their best abilities
3. Growth facilitated—more capital and better range of ability possible than in a single proprietorship
4. Flexibility—a partnership may perform any legal act without permission from the state
5. Relative freedom from government control and special taxation.

Disadvantages of the Partnership.
1. Unlimited liability for at least one partner
2. Unstable life

3. Difficulty of obtaining capital in large amounts, particularly through long-term loans
4. Firm bound by acts of one partner as an agent
5. Difficulty of disposing of partnership interest.

FORMATION OF A PARTNERSHIP

A partnership is ordinarily formed by a written or oral voluntary contract among the partners. To prevent misunderstanding, a written contract is desirable. Such an agreement, called the *articles of copartnership,* should clearly express the intentions of the partners relating to the rights and duties of each partner and give particular attention to such matters as the amount of investment to be made, limitations on withdrawals of funds, the ratios in which profits and losses are to be shared, and admission and withdrawal of partners.

LEGAL PROBLEMS OF A PARTNERSHIP

The relationship among partners gives rise to legal problems not found in other types of business organization. In the eyes of the law, a partnership is an association of individuals, and not an entity like the corporation. Ordinarily, legal actions must involve the individuals rather than the firm.

The *relationship of mutual agency* gives each partner the right to act as an agent for all the partners and to bind them by any acts that would reasonably appear to be within the scope of his authority. Each member of a partnership is individually liable for the debts of the firm except in the cases of limited partnerships, and even in such an instance, at least one partner must have unlimited liability.

KINDS OF PARTNERS

The legal status of partners varies not only among partnerships, but sometimes among the partners in the same enterprise. Some of the more common classes of partners are as follows:

1. *General partner.* A general, or active, partner is liable to an unlimited extent for the partnership debts and has a voice in the management.
2. *Limited partner.* A limited, or special, partner is liable to a limited extent for the partnership debts. An individual can have the status of a limited partner only under the restricted conditions expressly permitted by law.
3. *Silent partner.* A silent partner has a financial interest in the firm but does not participate in its management and is not known to be a partner.
4. *Secret partner.* A secret partner has a financial interest in the firm and actively participates in its management but is not known to be a partner
5. *Nominal partner.* A nominal partner has no financial interest in the firm but allows his name to appear as a partner and thereby assumes the unlimited liability of a general partner.

ADMISSION OF A NEW PARTNER

A new partnership results when an additional partner joins a partnership. The same accounting records may be continued, or new books may be required. There are two bases for the admission of a new partner: One represents the purchase of a part of existing partnership interests, and the other represents the investment of additional assets in the business. In either case, the accounting problem involved is to record the partners' capital accounts correctly.

Purchase of a Part of Existing Partnership Interests. An incoming partner may purchase his interest from one or more of the old partners, paying them directly without affecting the assets of the partnership. Regardless of the actual size of his investment, his capital account is credited with an amount agreed upon, which is deducted from the capital accounts of one or more of the old partners.

Investment of Additional Assets in the Enterprise. When an investment of an incoming partner is placed in the partnership, the amount is not paid directly to one or more of the partners; instead, the assets of the enterprise are increased by at least the amount of the investment. Following are five bases for recording the investment of such additional assets in the enterprise:

1. *Goodwill allowance to old partners.* Goodwill created by the old partnership is recorded by debiting the goodwill account and crediting the capital accounts of the old partners.

2. *Goodwill allowance to new partner.* Goodwill brought to the enterprise by the new partner is recorded by debiting the goodwill account and crediting the capital account of the new partner.

3. *Bonus to old partners.* If goodwill created by the old partnership is not recorded as an asset, the investment of the new partner is recorded by debiting assets for the total amount, crediting the old partners' capital accounts with the amount of the bonus, and crediting the new partner's capital account with the remainder.

4. *Bonus to new partner.* When goodwill brought to the enterprise by the new partner is not recorded as an asset, the investment of the new partner is recorded by debiting assets with the amount invested (excluding goodwill), debiting the capital accounts of the old partners with the amount of the bonus, and crediting the new partner's capital account with the total.

5. *Neither goodwill nor bonus recognized.* The investment of the new partner is recorded by debiting assets and crediting his capital account with the amount of the investment.

PROPRIETARY ACCOUNTS

In a partnership, two accounts are ordinarily kept for each partner. One is his capital account and the other is his personal, or drawing, or current, account.

The capital and personal accounts are maintained like those of the single proprietorship, referred to above.

DISPOSITION OF PROFIT AND LOSS

The balance of the income summary account is distributed to the partners in the ratio indicated by the copartnership agreement; or if no provision is made, profits and losses are shared equally among the partners. Each partner's share of the profit or loss is closed to his personal account or to his capital account in a manner similar to that employed in the single proprietorship.

Bases for Distribution of Profit and Loss. Following are various ways in which the copartnership agreement provides for the division of profits and losses:

1. Arbitrary (or fixed) ratio, including equal division
2. Investment ratio, including original investment, investment at certain dates, or average investment
3. Interest on investment and distribution of remainder on another basis
4. Salaries to partners and distribution of remainder on another basis
5. Any combination of the above bases.

DISSOLUTION

Dissolution of a partnership comes about when the copartnership agreement is terminated by an act of the parties, by automatic operation of the law, or by action of the courts.

Reasons for Partnership Dissolution. A partnership may be dissolved for the following reasons:

1. Accomplishment of the purpose for which the partnership was formed
2. Passage of a specific period of time or occurrence of a specified event
3. Decision to become incorporated
4. Sale of the firm
5. Admission of a new partner
6. Retirement of a partner

7. Death of a partner
8. Bankruptcy of a partner
9. Failure of the firm
10. Illegality
11. Declaration of war between the country in which the partnership was formed and a country in which one or more of the partners are citizens
12. Incapacity or insanity of a partner
13. Misconduct of a partner
14. Disagreement among the partners that cannot be settled, or unwillingness to continue the association
15. Inability to perform the work for which the partnership was formed.

Dissolution terminates a partnership, but it does not necessarily cause the discontinuance of the business. The business may be continued by a different partnership or another form of business organization.

Distribution of Partnership Assets. In the case of liquidation of a partnership, the assets are distributed in the following order:

1. Payment to creditors other than partners
2. Repayment to partners of loans or advances they have made to the partnership that do not constitute capital investment
3. Distribution to the partners of any profit or loss resulting from the liquidation
4. Return of the partners' investment as indicated by the final balance of each partner's capital account.

CHAPTER 14

Corporation

A *corporation,* as defined by Chief Justice Marshall in a famous decision (the Dartmouth College case) in 1819, "is an artificial being, invisible, intangible, and existing only in contemplation of law. Being a mere creature of law, it possesses only those properties which the charter of its creation confers upon it, either expressly, or as incidental to its very existence."

A corporation is a distinct legal entity, separate from the individuals who own it. A large part of the growth of the corporate form of business enterprise has occurred since the middle of the nineteenth century. It is the dominant form of organization for large-scale enterprises in the United States.

Some of the characteristics that distinguish a corporation from other forms of business organizations are: separate legal individuality and existence, charter granted by the state, proprietorship interest shown by shares of stock which are transferable units of proprietorship, limited liability of stockholders, continuity of existence, and limitation of action.

Advantages of the Corporation.
1. Limitation of the stockholder's liability to a fixed amount, usually the amount of his investment
2. Ownership readily transferable
3. Separate legal existence
4. Stability and relative permanence of existence
5. Ease of securing capital in large amounts and from many investors, through the issuance of various stocks and long-term bonds
6. Delegated authority. Centralized control secured when owners delegate authority to hired managers.

Disadvantages of the Corporation.
1. Activities limited by the charter
2. Manipulation—minority stockholders sometimes exploited
3. Extensive government regulation and burdensome local, state, and federal reports
4. Numerous and sometimes excessive taxes
5. Indirect reward when manager does not share in the profits.

FORMATION OF A CORPORATION

A corporation is usually formed by the authority of some state government. Corporations that do business in more than one state must comply with the federal laws regarding interstate commerce and with the state laws, which may vary considerably in the states in which they operate.

The procedure ordinarily required to form a corporation is, first, that subscriptions to capital stock must be taken and a tentative organization created, and second, that approval must be obtained from the Secretary of State in the state in which the corporation is to be formed. This approval is in the form of a charter for the corporation stating the powers and limitations of the particular enterprise.

LEGAL PROBLEMS OF A CORPORATION

A corporation is legally limited in its operations to those activities permitted by its charter. Care should be exercised, therefore, to keep a corporation's actions within the limits specified by its charter. Corporations generally are subject to more legal restrictions and government regulation than are other forms of business enterprise.

A corporation, being a distinct legal entity, may sue and be sued in its own name.

ORGANIZATION EXPENSE

Costs incurred in the creation of a corporation represent capital expenditures. They are capitalized by being debited to an asset account, organization expense. Presumably, the value of this asset will last as long as the corporation exists, because any similar corporation would have to meet similar costs to become established. The value of a large organization expense item may be questioned by readers of the balance sheet, however, and it is considered conservative practice for many kinds of business to write off the account early in the life of the corporation, perhaps over a period of five years, as permitted by the Internal Revenue Code.

PROPRIETARY ACCOUNTS

In a single proprietorship and a partnership, each owner has at least one account representing his investment in the business. If he has another proprietorship account, such as a current drawing account, it is usually closed into the permanent capital account at the close of an accounting period, as indicated in Chapter 13.

The proprietary accounts for a corporation consist principally of one capital stock account in the general ledger, or more if there are several classes of stock, and of at least one retained earnings account, formerly known as surplus. Details of the capital stock ownership are shown on the stubs of the capital stock certificates, and, in the larger enterprises, in separate capital stock ledgers, which are subsidiary to the general ledger account.

Capital stock is the evidence of ownership of a corporation. It is divided into equal shares, which are represented by capital stock certificates held by the owners (known as *stockholders*) and recorded as a total in the capital stock account. If there are several classes of stock, the shares in each class are uniform, but they differ from the shares in other classes.

The capital stock account does not change with ordinary

transfers of stock ownership from one holder to another, but is changed when either the number of shares outstanding or the valuation placed on each share is changed.

Control of a corporation is vested in its stockholders, who exercise their control by vote. Some classes of stock do not carry the voting privilege, and are known as *nonvoting stock*. Holders of *voting stock* may participate in stockholders' meetings, held annually or, when necessary, more often. At these meetings, stockholders receive reports on the operations of the enterprise, pass on important phases of its activities, and elect a small group from their number to represent them as *directors* in a somewhat more active and direct control of the business.

Stockholders may not withdraw profits from a corporation at will. They are entitled to their proportionate share only to the extent that dividends are declared by the directors.

CLASSES OF CAPITAL STOCK

There are two principal classes of capital stock, *common* and *preferred*. Many varieties exist within these classes, providing for different rights relating to income, control, and treatment in case of dissolution. If only one class of stock is issued, it is common stock, although it is usually called simply *capital stock*.

COMMON STOCK

Common stock represents the ownership of stockholders who have a residual claim on the assets of the corporation after all other claims have been met.

There may be more than one class of common stock, such as classes *A* and *B*. These differ in such matters as amount of control exercised over the corporation and share of the profits.

PREFERRED STOCK

Stock which has priority over other stock of the same company, either with respect to its share of profits or to its share of assets in case of dissolution, or both, is called preferred stock. Owners of preferred stock have the same rights as owners of common stock, in addition to the priority rights, unless otherwise specified. There is no guarantee, however, that dividends will be paid or that the investment itself will ultimately be repaid.

Cumulative Features. Stock which is preferred as to dividends is cumulative unless otherwise specified. All unpaid dividends on cumulative stock must be paid before earnings may be distributed to the holders of common stock. Preferred stock which indicates that it does not have the cumulative provision is *non-cumulative*. Preferred stock may be noncumulative for a specified period of time and then become cumulative.

Participation. After provision has been made for dividends on preferred stock at the stated rate, the holders of such stock may be entitled to share with the holders of common stock in any remaining amount available for dividends. In some instances, such participation becomes effective after a specified amount has been distributed to the holders of common stock. If preferred stock participates in the earnings beyond the stated dividend rate, it is called *participating;* if it is limited to the stated dividend rate, it is *nonparticipating*.

TYPES OF STOCK VALUE

Par Value. *Par value* of stock is a nominal figure given to shares of capital stock as stated in a corporation's charter and on its stock certificates. Par value has no necessary relation to the price of the stock. It may indicate the amount paid for the stock when originally issued, but stock can be issued originally at a price above par, or even below par when permitted by law.

Par-value stock is capital stock which has a par value, usually $100 a share. It is customary to show this value in a capital stock account. *No-par stock* is capital stock to which no par value has been assigned. No-par stock, if it has no stated value, is recorded in a capital stock account at the issuing price or prices.

Book Value. *Book value* of stock is the value per share of capital stock based on proprietorship. When there is only one class of capital stock, book value is determined by dividing total proprietorship (the excess of assets over liabilities) by the number of shares outstanding. When there are several classes of capital stock, the portion of proprietorship assignable to any one class is the basis for determining the book value of that class.

Market Value. *Market value* of stock is the price per share at which the stock is currently selling in the market.

Stated Value. *Stated value* of stock is the valuation per share placed on no-par stock by the stockholders or the board of directors. When stock has a stated value, that amount is properly shown in the capital stock account. Amounts in excess of stated value received from sales of the stock are credited to an account indicating that it is additional paid-in capital or capital in excess of stated value.

RECORDING SALE OF STOCK

There are two commonly accepted methods of recording a sale of capital stock. The method chosen should be adopted at the time the formation of the corporation is recorded in the accounting records. It is desirable, regardless of the method used, to place at the beginning of the journal at least a brief description of the new corporation. Sometimes, this description is rather extensive, including a copy of the charter and other documents required at the organization of the enterprise. Names of the accounts that record capital stock transactions vary somewhat at times, but the designations given below are generally acceptable.

If there are two or more classes of capital stock, separate accounts must be kept for them so that transactions relating to each class are clearly distinguishable. For instance, there should be separate accounts for subscriptions receivable, common, and for subscriptions receivable, preferred.

1. *Pro forma method.* When a bookkeeper employs the pro forma method, he makes the first journal entry relating to capital stock by debiting unissued capital stock account and crediting authorized capital stock with the entire amount of stock authorized by the charter. This entry is called the *pro forma entry.* The amount entered is the

total par value or the total stated value of the stock. The pro forma method cannot be used for no-par stock which has no stated value, but when following an alternative method, the number of shares authorized should be written as a memorandum in the capital stock account.

In the second entry, the bookkeeper debits subscriptions receivable and credits capital stock subscribed with the amount of subscriptions to capital stock received. There may be one such entry, or many. If the subscribers agree to pay more or less than par for the stock, subscriptions receivable account is debited with the amounts to be received, capital stock subscribed is credited with the par value of the stock to be issued, and the difference is credited to premium on stock if the price is above par, or debited to discount on stock if the price is below par.

Subscriptions receivable constitute an asset of the firm. They represent legally enforceable contracts with purchasers of capital stock. The capital stock subscribed account represents a liability of the firm to issue capital stock to the subscribers in accordance with their contracts.

In the third entry, the bookkeeper debits cash or other asset accounts, and credits subscriptions receivable with the amount received on the subscriptions. In the fourth entry, he debits capital stock subscribed and credits unissued capital stock with the amount of stock issued to subscribers.

This method has the merit of showing in the account balances the total amount of capital stock authorized by the corporation charter and the amount not yet issued.

2. *An alternative method.* The bookkeeper may begin his entries by debiting subscriptions receivable and crediting capital stock subscribed with the amount of subscriptions received, treating premium or discount on the capital stock as described under the pro forma method. He then debits cash, or other asset amounts, and credits subscriptions receivable with the amount received on the subscriptions. These entries are exactly like the second and third entries under the pro forma method. When stock is issued to the

subscribers, the amount is debited to capital stock subscribed and credited to capital stock.

PREMIUM AND DISCOUNT ON STOCK

Capital stock is issued occasionally for more or less than its par value. The amount received above par is a *premium*, which is credited to an account, premium on stock, or an account whose title has a similar meaning, such as capital in excess of par, additional paid-in capital, other paid-in capital, or additional capital. Where state laws permit the issue of stock for less than par, the amount received below par is a *discount* which is debited to an account, discount on stock.

Premium on stock should appear in the owners' equity section of a balance sheet as an addition to the par value of stock outstanding. It represents capital in excess of par value invested by the owners.

Discount on stock should appear on the balance sheet as a deduction from the par value of stock outstanding. It is not an asset, but measures the amount below par invested by the stockholders. A concern, having sold stock at a discount, may desire to close out the discount account so that it will not appear as a separate item on the balance sheet. Authorities generally disapprove of such a procedure, but it is encountered at times, when permitted by state law. The adjusting entry will debit paid-in capital, or retained earnings, and credit discount on stock.

No-par stock which has a stated value is often issued for more than that value, and if permitted by law, it may be issued for less than that value. The resulting premium or discount is handled like the premium or discount on par value stock. Instead of selling stock at less than stated value, however, a corporation probably would prefer to take the simple step of reducing the stated value.

As with other sections of the balance sheet, varying terms and arrangements are employed in reporting a corporation's paid-in capital. The following examples illustrate two such variations:

STOCKHOLDERS' EQUITY

Paid-in capital
Common stock, $20 par (40,000 shares
   authorized, 30,000 shares issued) $600,000
Capital in excess of par value   150,000 $750,000
From donations   24,000
From sale of treasury stock   9,000
   Total paid-in capital $783,000

CAPITAL

Contributed capital
Common stock, $20 par (40,000 shares
   authorized, 30,000 shares issued) $600,000
Additional paid-in capital   183,000
   Total contributed capital $783,000

RECORDS PECULIAR TO THE CORPORATION

In addition to the usual journals and ledgers kept by all types of business organizations, a corporation needs a minute book and stock certificates and may use other special records relating to its proprietary accounts. Some of these records are as follows:

1. *Minute book.* A record of the proceedings of the meetings of stockholders and of the board of directors
2. *Stock certificate book.* This book contains serially numbered blank stock certificates, to be issued to stockholders, and attached stubs, to be retained as a record of stock outstanding. When a certificate is canceled, the usual practice is to attach it to its stub.
3. *Stock subscription book.* A book containing the subscription blanks on which subscribers contract for purchase of capital stock
4. *Subscribers' cash receipts journal.* A special cash book which shows the amounts of payments on stock subscriptions
5. *Subscribers' ledger.* A subsidiary ledger which contains the individual subscribers' accounts and is controlled by the general ledger account, subscriptions receivable
6. *Stockholders' ledger,* or *capital stock ledger.* A record of

the capital stock outstanding, which contains a separate account for each stockholder showing the number of shares he owns and his stock certificate serial numbers and dates

7. *Stock transfer journal.* A journal used to record the transfer of stock from one stockholder to another.

TREASURY STOCK

Treasury stock is capital stock which has been issued and paid for in full and later reacquired by the issuing corporation as a result of purchase or donation. Methods of accounting for treasury stock vary. The following are representative procedures.

When treasury stock is purchased, the amount of the purchase price is debited to the account, treasury stock, according to one plan, known as the cost basis. When sold, treasury stock account is credited with the amount paid for the stock, and any difference between that amount and the selling price is debited or credited to an account such as paid-in capital from sales of treasury stock.

Some accountants prefer to record a purchase of treasury stock by debiting treasury stock account at par or stated value. If the purchase price is greater than par or stated value, the excess is debited to an account such as premium on treasury stock, or paid-in capital. If the stock is purchased at a discount, the amount below par or stated value is credited to discount on treasury stock, or paid-in capital.

A purchase of treasury stock is recorded with a credit to cash, or some other asset account, at the amount of the purchase price, but if such stock is received as a gift, the par or stated value is credited to donated capital. When no-par stock without a stated value is acquired, it is recorded in a treasury stock account at cost if purchased, and probably at the average selling price of the stock if received as a gift.

Accounts for premium and discount on treasury stock purchases are closed into paid-in capital at the end of the accounting period, or, in order to avoid a debit balance in paid-in capital, they may be closed to retained earnings. Gains or losses on disposition of treasury stock are transferred in the same manner to paid-in capital or retained earnings.

Treasury stock is treated by some corporations as an asset, a temporary investment held for resale. Another view, generally preferred, is that treasury stock represents a reduction of capital stock outstanding and should be shown on the balance sheet as a deduction from the amount of stock issued.

DONATED STOCK

Donated stock is treasury stock which has been donated by stockholders. Usually, the purpose is to permit the corporation to sell the stock for needed working capital.

The entry recording the gift debits treasury stock, or donated stock, and credits donated capital with the par or stated value of the stock, or with its average selling price if it has no par or stated value. Sales of the stock at less than the amount at which it is recorded in the treasury stock account, decrease the donated capital; sales at a higher figure increase it. Donated capital represents additional investment in the business and should not be confused with retained earnings.

WATERED STOCK

Watered stock is capital stock of any class which has been issued at par or stated value in excess of the fair value of the assets received for it. The amount of water in the stock is the amount by which the assets received for it are overvalued on the balance sheet.

SURPLUS

Surplus, as the term formerly appeared on balance sheets, customarily represented the excess of proprietorship over the capital stock of a corporation. If proprietorship was less than the capital stock, the deficit was indicated in the surplus account with a debit balance and on the balance sheet as a deficit to be deducted from the other proprietorship accounts.

Surplus usually was divided into *capital surplus* and *earned surplus,* with perhaps several accounts in each group, such as paid-in surplus, donated surplus, revaluation surplus, appropriated earned surplus, and unappropriated earned surplus. The capital surplus accounts would include all additions to the proprietorship of the corporation that did not represent earnings properly credited to earned surplus or additional capital stock properly credited to a capital stock account. Earned surplus consisted of undistributed earnings of a corporation.

Criticisms of the term *surplus* were widespread, stressing the fact that it was not descriptive enough and often left the users of a balance sheet in doubt as to its exact meaning. As a result, surplus as a balance sheet item has been replaced in recent years and now is encountered only rarely in financial reports. Other more informative titles are favored, such as paid-in capital instead of paid-in surplus, and retained earnings instead of earned surplus.

A balance sheet should always reveal proprietorship in its principal component parts. When more details seem to be required for a clearer interpretation of the figures, separate listings of subdivisions of the parts are often helpful. Classified according to source, a corporation's proprietorship accounts other than capital stock can be divided into three groups, as follows:

1. *Contributed capital.* Accounts in this group should appear separately on the balance sheet if amounts are substantial. They have resulted from transactions involving such items as premium on sales of capital stock (*paid-in capital*), assessments against stockholders, forfeitures of stock subscription deposits and rights, gifts of property or of the corporations' own stock (*donated capital*), and profit on purchases and sales of treasury stock.

2. *Appraisal capital.* Occasionally, an enterprise will decide to record a large unrealized increase in the market value of an asset, although such a procedure is not acceptable to most accountants. The account for the property is debited

with the estimated amount of increase, while the credit is placed in an account such as appraisal capital, capital arising from revaluation of assets, or capital from appreciation of assets.

3. *Retained earnings.* This title represents an accumulation of undistributed earnings. The following are its two important subdivisions:

(1) *Appropriated retained earnings,* representing portions of past earnings set aside in separate accounts for special purposes, such as a reserve for sinking fund or a reserve for contingencies, and (2) *unappropriated net earnings,* showing amounts available for dividends.

Appropriated retained earnings are known also as restricted retained earnings. Formerly, they were classified as surplus reserves. Unappropriated retained earnings appear under various titles such as undistributed retained earnings, accumulated earnings, undivided profits, and, on rare occasions, as free surplus or earned surplus.

DISPOSITION OF PROFIT AND LOSS

A corporation's net profit or loss for an accounting period is transferred from the income summary account to the retained earnings account when the books are closed. The present tendency is to favor the *clean surplus* theory, explained in Chapter 3, which records in the income summary account all gains or losses incurred during the current accounting period, whether resulting from ordinary, normal, recurring business operations, or from nonrecurring extraordinary events, and including even an occasional adjustment affecting the profit of a prior year.

Dividends declared and appropriations of retained earnings are usually debited to retained earnings, but some accountants prefer to debit them to income summary, or net income account, before the balance is transferred to retained earnings.

Accumulated profits in the retained earnings account are reduced by: (1) losses, (2) transfers to appropriated retained earnings accounts (formerly called surplus reserves), and (3) dividends declared.

DIVIDENDS

A *dividend* ordinarily is a proportional distribution of earnings to the stockholders. It is not an expense. The directors alone have the right to declare dividends. A stockholder may claim a share of the profits only to the extent that dividends have been declared.

Payment of a cash dividend out of contributed capital is legal under some circumstances but is usually to be avoided because it is, in effect, a return of capital, not profits. A stock dividend out of contributed capital merely has the effect on the balance sheet of shifting the amount of the dividend from the contributed capital account to capital stock.

Dividends Out of Capital. If a dividend is paid in excess of the amount of retained earnings, the excess is actually a return of invested capital. It is unlawful, generally, to pay dividends out of capital except: (1) when a corporation goes out of business and distributes the proceeds from sales of its assets to creditors and stockholders as *liquidating dividends,* and (2) when an enterprise dealing in wasting assets, such as a mine or a timber tract, desires to distribute to its stockholders not only the profits made, but also portions of the invested capital recovered from sales of the product and not required for reinvestment by the company.

Any dividend that impairs capital should be identified clearly so that the recipients will know that they are receiving a return of part of their invested capital.

Dividends Out of Earnings. Dividends paid out of earnings can be classified conveniently into four groups, as follows:
1. *Cash dividends.* The great majority of dividends are paid in cash.
2. *Commodity dividends.* Occasionally, this form of dividend, known also as a *dividend in kind,* is declared, payable in assets of the corporation other than cash.
3. *Scrip dividends.* Corporations facing a temporary shortage

of cash sometimes issue dividends in scrip, or notes, payable at a future date. If dividends have been paid regularly, this method prevents a break in the continuity of the payments, called *passing* a dividend. Ordinarily, however, the practice of issuing scrip dividends is not advisable.

4. *Stock dividends.* A dividend need not require the reduction of proprietorship and the disposal of assets. It can be paid in stock of the corporation if there is unissued stock or treasury stock available. Usually a stock dividend is declared out of retained earnings, with the result that the amount of the dividend is transferred on the books of the corporation from retained earnings available for dividends to a capital stock account, without a change in the total proprietorship or the total assets. The accumulated earnings so transferred become a part of the permanent invested capital of the enterprise.

Entries to Record Dividends. The declaration and payment of a dividend can be journalized in a simple manner, as follows:

(1)

Retained Earnings	5,000.00	
Dividends Payable		5,000.00

To record declaration of 5% cash dividend, payable June 25, 19—, to stockholders of record June 15, 19—.

(2)

Dividends Payable	5,000.00	
Cash		5,000.00

To record payment of dividend.

The dividends payable account is a liability of the corporation. If a dividend is to be paid in property, scrip, or stock instead of cash, the entry to record the declaration can be similar to the first entry above, with a distinctive title, such as stock dividend payable, if desired, and the proper description. Payment of such a dividend will require an entry similar to the second entry above, with a credit to the proper account.

CONTRIBUTED CAPITAL AND RETAINED EARNINGS ON THE BALANCE SHEET

When more than one class of capital stock is outstanding, the various classes should be shown separately on the balance sheet. If there is any unissued stock or treasury stock, the amounts ordinarily should be disclosed in the stockholders' equity section of the balance sheet. All other corporation proprietorship accounts should appear in the stockholders' equity section also, grouped according to types. Then the resulting total will represent the entire proprietorship claims of the owners.

PSEUDO CORPORATION

The pseudo, or Sub-Chapter S, corporation is a company organized under state laws as a regular corporation but which has elected to meet certain requirements and obtain some privileges under Sub-Chapter S of the Internal Revenue Code.

In brief, a pseudo corporation is a small company that for federal income tax purposes passes its profits and losses through to its stockholders in a manner similar to the way profits and losses are handled and taxed in a partnership. The advantages may be limited to the federal income tax.

CHAPTER 15

Bonds, Funds, and Reserves

BONDS AN EVIDENCE OF INDEBTEDNESS

A bond is a promise, under seal, to pay a specified sum of money at a definite future date, usually with interest at a specified rate payable periodically.

There is little significant difference between bonds and promissory notes. A bond is a more formal document than a note. It must be executed under seal, while a note need not be. The expression *under seal* means that a signature is accompanied by the word "seal" or by some other symbol. Under some laws, a contract under seal possesses greater force than an ordinary contract. A bond ordinarily matures after ten, twenty, or more years, while most notes are made for short terms. Both bondholders and the owners of a corporation's promissory notes are creditors of the issuing corporation, and not owners as are the stockholders.

A bond is a unit in a series of similar bonds. The face value (par value or principal) is commonly $1,000, but other denominations are not unusual. Interest paid on a bond is a fixed amount determined by the stated rate and the face value, regardless of the price at which the bond is sold.

TYPES OF BONDS

Bonds differ in their provisions in a bewildering variety of ways. These variations provide bases for many types of classification, five of which are given here, together with brief descriptions of various bonds. Any specific bond can be classified under each of the following types.

Purpose for Which Bonds Are Issued.

1. Adjustment bonds, issued to readjust the amount of debt
2. Consolidated bonds, issued to replace several bond issues and simplify the debt structure
3. Funding bonds, issued to consolidate unfunded debt, or debt represented by notes and accounts payable
4. Refunding bonds, issued to replace an existing funded debt, or debt represented by bonds
5. Purchase money bonds, issued in part or full payment for property purchased
6. Construction, extension, and improvement bonds, issued to obtain funds for purposes specified.

Nature of the Issuing Authority.

1. Governmental bonds, issued by federal and state governments and their instrumentalities
2. Commercial bonds, issued by railroads, public utilities, and financial and industrial enterprises.

Character of Security of Principal.

1. *Unsecured* bonds. These bonds have no assets pledged as security for their payment. They are merely general obligations of the issuing company. They are generally called debentures, or debenture bonds.
2. *Secured* bonds. These bonds have certain assets, or a guarantee, pledged as security for their payment. They can be classified as follows:
   a. Mortgage bonds, usually secured by a mortgage on real estate
   b. Collateral trust bonds, usually secured by a lien on bonds or other securities, or personal property
   c. Equipment obligations, usually secured by a lien on the equipment for the purchase of which they were issued
   d. Guaranteed bonds, for which the security is the guaranty of another company.

Manner of Interest Payment.

1. Registered bonds, each of which bears the owner's name,

is non-negotiable, and provides that interest payments be made by check direct to the registered owner

2. Coupon bonds, or bearer bonds, each of which is payable to bearer, is negotiable, and is accompanied by coupons to be cashed on interest payment dates in lieu of direct interest payments from the issuing corporation

3. Registered coupon bonds, each of which bears the owner's name, is non-negotiable, and is accompanied by coupons payable to bearer for the interest payments.

Manner of Payment of Principal.

1. Serial bonds, providing for maturity of parts of the issue periodically

2. Straight bonds, or term bonds, providing for maturity of the entire issue at one time

3. Callable bonds, or redeemable bonds, subject to call for redemption by the issuing corporation prior to maturity

4. Sinking fund bonds, requiring the issuing corporation to set aside a sinking fund out of which to pay the bonds at maturity

5. Convertible bonds, permitting the exchange of the bonds for other securities of the issuing corporation at the option of the bondholders and according to the terms specified.

BOND PRICES

There are a number of factors that determine the price at which a bond is sold. One of the most important and most obvious factors is the security of the bond, which is measured by the prospect of regularity of interest payments and ultimate repayment of the principal. When bonds of equal security are compared, the most important factor in determining price is the interest rate.

The *nominal* interest rate is the rate stated in the bond. It is the rate at which interest payments are made, based on the face value of the bond, regardless of its selling price. The nominal interest rate is also known as the *coupon* rate and the *stated* rate.

The *effective* interest rate is the rate of return based on the actual price at which the bond was transferred. The effective interest rate is also known as the *yield* rate and the *effective* rate. If a bond sells at par, the nominal and effective rates are the same.

Premium on Bonds. If the nominal rate on a bond is higher than the *market* rate of interest (the rate of return which investors in the open market are willing to accept at a given time on that type of investment), the bond will sell for more than face value, and the difference between the selling price and par is *premium*.

The premium on bonds payable is a deferred credit to interest expense. Each interest payment will be at the coupon rate and will include in part interest cost and in part a return of a portion of the premium. The amount of premium received ordinarily should be written off, or amortized, over the life of the bonds.

Discount on Bonds. If the nominal rate on a bond is lower than the market rate of interest, the bond will sell for less than face value, and the difference between the selling price and par is *discount*.

The discount on bonds payable is a deferred charge to interest expense. Sometimes it appears on the assets side on the balance sheet as a deferred charge. A preferable treatment is to show it as a valuation account offset against bonds payable. The amount of the discount ordinarily should be amortized over the life of the bonds.

The nominal rate and the effective rate of a bond are seldom identical. This is due principally to fluctuations in the market rate of interest. The result is that most bonds are sold at either more or less than their face value.

A corporation might prefer to issue bonds with a nominal interest rate lower than the market rate, causing the bonds to sell at a discount, in order to make the interest cost seem lower than it would be if the same bonds bore a nominal rate higher than the market rate and sold at a premium. On the other hand, an enterprise such as a public school district, wishing to maintain a record that its occasional bond issues always sell at a premium, will establish the nominal interest rate for a new issue at a slightly higher figure than the market rate forecast for the date of issue. The nominal rate, however, does not control the actual interest cost, as determined by the effective rate, because proper accounting methods require that either a premium or a discount should be amortized in order to make the effective rate equal to the market rate at the time the bonds are sold.

DISPOSITION OF PREMIUM AND DISCOUNT ON BONDS

A bond generally requires payment of its face value at maturity, and any premium or discount associated with it should be written off by that time.

Amortization of bond premium or discount is the periodic writing off of the premium or discount over the life of the bonds. The balance remaining in a bond premium or discount account at any time is the *unamortized* balance. Frequently, the titles *unamortized premium on bonds payable* and *unamortized discount on bonds payable* appear in the records.

Book value of a bond is the sum of the face value and the unamortized premium, or the difference between the face value and the unamortized discount.

If bonds are sold above face value, the premium should appear on the credit side of a premium on bonds payable account. Entries to amortize the premium are made periodically, preferably at the time of each interest payment. When such an entry is made, the amount to be written off, as determined by the amortization method adopted, is debited to premium on bonds payable account and credited to interest expense account. This entry reduces the unamortized bond premium, and at the same time reduces the interest cost from the total coupon amount to the approximate amount it should be as determined by the effective rate of the bonds.

If bonds are sold for less than face value, the discount should appear on the debit side of a discount on bonds payable account. An entry to record amortization of the discount will debit interest expense account and credit discount on bonds payable account with the amount to be written off. This reduces the unamortized discount and increases the interest cost above the total coupon amount to the approximate figure indicated by the effective rate of the bonds.

Any variations in the procedures for amortizing premium or discount on bonds should achieve essentially the same effects. The amortization is sometimes recorded with the interest payment in one compound journal entry, as described later in this chapter.

Disposition of premium or discount on bonds is illustrated in the following examples:

1. *Straight-line amortization.* The simplest plan of amortization is to write off an equal amount of the premium or discount applicable to each bond at each interest payment date. This is called the *straight-line method,* or the *bonds outstanding method.* It is easy to understand and simple to operate and, therefore, is widely used. However, it is not as accurate as the interest method.

2. *Interest method of amortization.* The method which provides for systematic writing off of bond premium or discount and at the same time achieves the most accurate record of interest cost, is the *interest method.* Under this plan, an issuing corporation may compute the amount of interest cost on its bonds at any time by multiplying the book value of the bonds at that time by the effective rate applicable to them. The difference between the interest so computed and the nominal interest is the amount of premium or discount to be amortized. Interest cost changes at each interest payment date because of changes in the book value of the bonds brought about by amortization.

   Present value of the bonds at each interest payment date may be computed by mathematical formulas, and the difference between the values at the beginning and end of an interest period is the amount of premium or discount to be amortized. This is a variation of the interest method and should produce the same results as the application of the effective rate.

3. *Bond table method of amortization.* Bond tables are published which give the present value of bonds on their interest payment dates at various nominal interest rates and various effective interest rates. Bond tables facilitate the

computation of amortization of premium or discount by providing the present value at interest payment dates and eliminating the need for computations by mathematical formulas as indicated above.

4. *Use of amortization schedules.* Amortization schedules may be prepared for each bond issue at the time the bonds are issued. These schedules should include information desired at each interest payment date, such as the amount of interest to be paid, the amount to be charged to the interest expense account, the amount of premium or discount to be amortized, and the unamortized balance of premium or discount. The computations for amortization of bond premium or discount over the life of the bonds can be made at the time the bonds are issued and entered in an amortization schedule by interest payment dates. At the time of interest payments, it is not necessary to make any additional computations, but only to refer to the amortization schedule for the information necessary for proper journal entries.

ACCOUNTING FOR BONDS

The following discussion deals with the records for bonds payable. Assuming cash transactions, a representative method of making the entries is given, but numerous variations are found. No discussion of the records to be kept by the holder of bonds is undertaken here, since the problems are somewhat similar, differing principally in the fact that the bonds are a liability of the issuing corporation and an asset of the bondholder.

Bonds maturing more than a year in the future constitute fixed or long-term liabilities of the issuing corporation. The same bonds will be either current or other assets of the bondholder, depending upon whether he intends to hold them as temporary investments or as long-term investments.

A journal entry to record the sale of bonds or the payment of interest on them, is influenced by the amount received for the bonds, whether face value or more or less than face value.

Recording Sale of Bonds.

1. *Sale at par.* When bonds are sold for their face value, the journal entry to record the sale is a debit to cash and a credit to bonds payable for the amount of the bonds.

2. *Sale at a premium.* When bonds are sold for more than their face value, the journal entry to record the sale is a debit to cash for the total amount received, a credit to bonds payable for the face value of the bonds issued, and a credit to premium on bonds payable for the difference, which is the amount of the premium received.

3. *Sale at a discount.* When bonds are sold for less than their face value, the journal entry to record the sale is a debit to cash for the amount received, a debit to discount on bonds payable for the difference between the amount received and the face value of the bonds issued, and a credit to bonds payable for the face value of the bonds issued.

This discussion has omitted the *pro forma entry,* preferred by some accountants, by which unissued bonds payable would be debited and authorized bonds payable credited for the face value of the bonds to be issued. If the pro forma method were used, a sale of bonds would be credited to unissued bonds payable to reduce that account.

Expenses relating to the issuance of bonds, such as printing and registration expenses and legal fees, are properly chargeable to a bond premium or discount account.

Recording Interest Payments.

1. *On bonds sold at par.* A journal entry to record the payment of interest on bonds sold at par consists of a debit to interest expense and a credit to cash for the amount paid.

2. *On bonds sold at a premium.* When the payment of interest on bonds sold at a premium is journalized, a compound entry will debit interest expense for the difference between the amount paid and the portion of premium to be amortized at that time, debit premium on bonds payable for the amount of amortization, and credit cash for the amount paid, which is at the nominal interest rate.

3. *On bonds sold at a discount.* When the payment of interest on bonds sold at a discount is journalized, a compound entry will consist of a debit to interest expense for the sum of

the amount paid and the portion of discount to be amortized at that time, a credit to discount on bonds payable for the amount of amortization, and a credit to cash for the amount paid, which is at the nominal interest rate.

Recording Principal Payments. When a payment of the principal of bonds payable is made, the journal entry to record such payment is a debit to bonds payable and a credit to cash. In some cases, the record of the last interest payment and the payment of the bonds will be combined. If this is done, a compound journal entry is used, which is merely a combination of the entry for the payment of the principal, the entry for the payment of interest, and the writing off of any remaining premium or discount.

Records. The issuing corporation should keep such records as would be necessitated by the nature of the bond issue. If the bond issue is composed of coupon bonds, there is no need, ordinarily, for special records beyond the files of correspondence and contracts and the customary entries in journals and the general ledger. If, however, registered bonds are sold, either a bonds payable register, or a bonds payable subsidiary ledger, or both, must be maintained, in order to have a record of the bondholders.

FUNDS

In ordinary usage, the term *funds* has several meanings. Frequently, in a narrow sense, it is used as a synonym for cash as in the case of a check dishonored, or not paid, by a bank because of "insufficient funds." It also covers the intermediate concept of working capital, or current assets minus current liabilities. In the broadest sense, the term funds encompasses all financial resources of an enterprise. The statement of changes in financial position, or funds statement, discussed in the next chapter, deals with the changes in a firm's financial resources that occur during an accounting period.

The term *fund* (singular) embraces cash and other assets, and sometimes related liabilities, set aside for a specific purpose. The principal purpose of a fund is usually to provide assets with which to meet a future need that is either known definitely in advance or can be predicted with reasonable accuracy. A university, for example, or a city will have several funds, each accounted for separately, and each, except the general fund, established and maintained for limited specific purposes.

A balance sheet for a city's special revenue fund created for a distinct purpose, such as support for a city museum, probably will contain the following types of accounts: assets, consisting of cash and taxes receivable (less allowance for uncollectible taxes); liabilities, consisting of vouchers payable; appropriated surplus, consisting of a reserve for encumbrances; and unappropriated surplus, or a balancing figure.

Most enterprises maintain at least a petty cash fund, and many have other funds such as those listed below.

CLASSES OF FUNDS

The more important classes of funds established by business enterprises are as follows:

1. *Funds for the acquisition of fixed assets.* One type is the *plant extension fund,* which is used in conjunction with an appropriated retained earnings account such as reserve, or appropriation, for plant extension. In this way, the management is assured that in accordance with a definite plan, assets will be set aside to pay for the expansion of the plant.

2. A *petty cash,* or *imprest, fund,* as previously explained, consists of cash set aside to take care of small miscellaneous expenditures which can be made most readily in cash.

3. *Branch funds* usually consist of cash sent to branches to facilitate their operation.

4. *Bond sinking funds* are used for the redemption of long-term liabilities. Such a fund is often created in accordance with the contract that exists between the enterprise and long-term creditors. It consists of cash or other assets which will be utilized to liquidate the obligation. The funds will be held by an impartial trustee, if so required by the bond contract.

5. *Miscellaneous funds* are established for various specific

purposes, depending upon the needs of a particular enterprise.

RESERVES

Reserve is a term which formerly appeared in numerous account titles. It was used in so many ways that the reader of a balance sheet was often puzzled as to its exact meaning. The term still appears on balance sheets, to a limited extent, principally to name appropriations of retained earnings, such as reserve for contingencies; but even there the term *appropriation* is preferred by many accountants. Other terms, including *allowance,* now widely used, have practically eliminated the use of *reserve* in other account titles. There are three types of accounts, formerly called reserves. They are: contra asset accounts, accrued liabilities, and appropriations of retained earnings.

Contra Asset Accounts. A *contra asset account,* often called an *allowance,* is an account which contains the accumulated periodic entries recording estimated decreases in the valuation of an asset. The title *allowance* is more precise, and therefore less confusing, than *reserve* for this type of account, as indicated in Chapter 9. Occasionally, *provision* appears as part of the title of such an account, but the term is not used widely. When recording depreciation and depletion, the term *accumulated* is applied frequently. This type of allowance permits the related asset account to retain unchanged its record of the original, or historic, cost of the asset. A *contra asset* account is an *offset,* or *asset valuation,* account. Examples are:

1. Allowance for bad debts
2. Allowance for depreciation (or accumulated depreciation)
3. Allowance for depletion.

Accrued Liabilities. An *allowance,* or *appropriation,* for a liability is an account which discloses the actual or estimated amount of an accrued liability. It is recorded with a corresponding debit to an expense account. It is properly termed an *accrued liability.* Examples other than those given in Chapter 9 are:

1. Accrued compensation insurance payable
2. Accrued taxes payable.

Appropriations of Retained Earnings. A reserve created from retained earnings is, in effect, a subdivision of retained earnings set aside for a particular purpose. It is used when management wishes to decrease the amount available for dividends and, for the present, to retain within the enterprise the earnings so segregated. It is shown on a balance sheet in the proprietorship section. Examples of this type of *reserve,* or *appropriation,* are:

1. Appropriation for contingencies
2. Appropriation for plant expansion
3. Appropriation for retirement of long-term debt (or appropriation for bond sinking fund)
4. Appropriation for retirement of preferred stock.

Terms such as *secret reserves* and *hidden reserves* appear occasionally in financial discussions, but they do not refer to a specific reserve account. They indicate, rather, an understatement of proprietorship. This understatement is accomplished by undervaluing or omitting an asset, or overvaluing a liability. The presence of a secret reserve causes erroneous values to be shown on the financial statements and conceals from stockholders and other interested persons the full value of the proprietorship.

Reserves and *funds* are accounting terms that occasionally have been confusing. The term *reserve* sometimes is employed incorrectly to refer to a fund consisting of assets set aside for some particular purpose. Both a fund and a reserve, appropriation, or allowance, relating to the same matter, are required simultaneously at times. An example is a bond sinking fund and an appropriation for sinking fund.

Plans for the bond sinking fund expect it to have sufficient assets to pay the bonds at maturity, the assets having been acquired by periodic transfers of stipulated amounts of cash plus earnings that investments made by the fund have produced. The appropriation for sinking fund account has an amount transferred to it each year from retained earnings. That amount is equal to the additions that year to the sinking fund, thus making equal totals for the asset account, sinking fund, and the proprietorship account, appropriation for sinking fund. Fund accounts and appropriated retained earnings accounts do not, however, always need to be associated; frequently, one of them appears on a balance sheet without the other.

ACCOUNTING FOR RESERVES OR ALLOWANCES

Journal Record. When a reserve, or allowance, is established or increased, a journal entry is made to credit the proper account. For a contra asset account, the corresponding debit is to an appropriate expense account. For a liability appropriation, commonly called an accrued liability, the debit also is placed in an expense account. For an appropriation of retained earnings, the debit is to the retained earnings account, known also as retained earnings unappropriated.

Balance Sheet Presentation. A contra asset account should appear on the balance sheet as a deduction from the asset to which it relates. The difference is the book value of the asset. Liability appropriations, being accrued liabilities, belong in the current liabilities section. Retained earnings appropriations, or reserves, should be shown as part of capital in the proprietorship section on the balance sheet.

ACCOUNTING FOR FUNDS

An entry to establish or increase a fund is made by debiting the fund account and crediting cash. When a fund is established for the purpose of acquiring fixed assets, an entry may be made at the same time to establish or increase appropriated capital by debiting retained earnings unappropriated and crediting a reserve account such as appropriation for plant extension.

If a fund is to be increased by interest earned by the assets of the fund, such increase is recorded by debiting the fund account, or the fund's cash account, if kept separately, and crediting an appropriate income account.

When the assets held in the fund are converted into the assets for which the fund was established, as in the case of a building fund, or used to pay a bonded debt, when dealing with a sinking fund, the net result in the records will be a debit to the account for the new assets in one situation, and a debit to the proper liability account in the other case, offset by a credit to the fund account.

A fund, such as a sinking fund, sometimes has slightly more or less cash than it will need at the time it is closed. An excess is returned to the company's regular operating cash account by debiting cash and crediting sinking fund. If the cash in the fund is not sufficient, the amount needed is transferred to the fund by a debit to the sinking fund account and a credit to cash.

At the time the fund account is closed, any retained earnings appropriation maintained in connection with it should be closed by a debit to the appropriation account and a credit to retained earnings unappropriated.

In the opinion of some accountants, funds should be shown on the balance sheet in a special classification between current and fixed assets. Others prefer to place a fund, such as a building fund, among the fixed assets.

CHAPTER 16

Funds Statement and Cash Flow

THE FUNDS STATEMENT

The *statement of changes in financial position,* or *funds statement,* formerly appeared only occasionally in financial reports. In recent years, it has come into such widespread use as a management tool and as a statement of disclosure that now it is considered to be one of the basic features required in most financial reports of business entities. It ranks in importance next to the balance sheet and the income statement.

FUNDS-FLOW ANALYSIS

A funds statement indicates the flow of funds of a firm, disclosing the sources from which funds were acquired during the accounting period covered by the report and the disposition made of them. The statement supplements the information given by the balance sheet and the income statement, throwing additional light on the financial strength or weakness of the firm.

DEVELOPMENT OF THE STATEMENT

The funds statement has been discussed and gradually developed in accounting literature over a number of years, appearing with a variety of forms and titles. Some of the various titles have been: statement of changes in financial position, funds statement, funds-flow statement, statement of source and application of funds, application of funds statement, where-got-where-gone statement, sources and uses of working capital, summary of changes in working capital, analysis of working capital changes, and statement of resources provided and applied.

CONTENTS OF THE STATEMENT

Material covered by the funds statement formerly was confined, generally, to changes in working capital (working capital being defined as current assets minus current liabilities, or net current assets). A broader "all financial resources" concept of funds, now widely employed, requires that the funds statement deal with all significant financial transactions undertaken by the firm during the period covered by the report, regardless of whether they affect working capital. Examples include the exchange of noncurrent assets for other noncurrent assets, or for bonds payable, or for capital stock; the payment of a noncurrent debt by the issuance of capital stock; and so on. The statement, therefore, should disclose clearly not only funds provided by operations and other changes in working capital, but all transactions of a material amount, however financed.

COMPARATIVE BALANCE SHEET

A *comparative balance sheet,* usually in condensed form, provides the basis for a funds statement when accompanied by sufficient information to explain the changes it discloses. Following is an example:

AJAX CORPORATION

COMPARATIVE BALANCE SHEET
AUGUST 31, CURRENT YEAR, AND AUGUST 31, PRECEDING YEAR

| | August 31 | | Differences | |
Assets	Current Year	Preceding Year	Debit	Credit
Cash	$ 74,000	$ 80,000		$ 6,000
Receivables (Net)	122,000	166,000		44,000
Inventories	390,000	380,000	$ 10,000	
Land	30,000	19,000	11,000	
Buildings and equipment	325,000	290,000	35,000	
Accumulated depreciation (buildings & equipment)	(83,000)	(69,000)	(14,000)	
	$858,000	$866,000		
Liabilities and Capital				
Accounts payable	$ 89,000	$134,000	45,000	
Mortgage payable	—	15,000	15,000	
Bonds payable	136,000	70,000		66,000
Capital stock, preferred 5%	—	50,000	50,000	
Capital stock, common, par $100	410,000	400,000		10,000
Paid in capital in excess of par value of common stock	155,000	150,000		5,000
Retained earnings	68,000	47,000		21,000
	$858,000	$866,000	$152,000	$152,000

Additional information is furnished, as follows:

1. A parcel of land which cost $5,000 was sold for $18,000 cash.

2. Additional land was purchased for $16,000, for which bonds payable were issued at par value.

3. Equipment was purchased and paid for with cash amounting to $35,000.

4. The mortgage payable balance of $15,000 was paid by issuing common capital stock having a par value of $10,000 and a market value of $15,000.

5. Preferred capital stock amounting to $50,000 was purchased and retired, exchanging for it a like amount of bonds payable at par.

6. Dividends of $28,000 were declared and paid.

7. The following highly condensed income statement explains the $21,000 increase in retained earnings:

AJAX CORPORATION

INCOME STATEMENT
FOR THE YEAR ENDED AUGUST 31, 19--

Sales		$2,500,000
Cost of goods sold		
Opening inventory	$ 380,000	
Purchases	1,500,000	
Cost of goods available for sale	$1,880,000	
Less closing inventory	390,000	
Cost of goods sold		1,490,000
Gross profit on sales		$1,010,000
Operating expenses (including $14,000 depreciation of building and equipment		974,000
Net income from operations		$ 36,000
Profit on sale of land		13,000
Total net income		$ 49,000
Dividends declared		28,000
Earnings retained		$ 21,000

STATEMENT OF CHANGES IN FINANCIAL POSITION

Based on the foregoing information, a funds statement for the Ajax Corporation is presented here. Accountants have not settled on a standard form for the statement, but the intention always should be to report clearly the sources from which funds have been acquired and the uses made of them.

In the following illustration, a schedule of changes in working capital accompanies the funds statement to explain the $5,000 increase in working capital. Such a schedule is not believed to be essential, however, and frequently is omitted from a report containing a funds statement.

A funds statement occasionally includes total sales and the deductions of cost of goods sold and operating expenses, which are shown above in the Ajax Corporation income statement. Others begin with net operating income, as shown on the illustrated funds statement.

AJAX CORPORATION

STATEMENT OF CHANGES IN FINANCIAL POSITION
FOR THE YEAR ENDED AUGUST 31, 19--

Sources of funds		
Operations		
Net income, exclusive of $13,000 gain on sale of land	$36,000	
Add expenses not requiring funds		
Depreciation of buildings and equipment	14,000	$ 50,000
Sale of land for cash		18,000
Issuance of bonds payable at par		
for purchase of land		16,000
for preferred capital stock to be retired		50,000
Issuance of 100 shares of common stock at $150 to pay balance due on mortgage payable		15,000
Total funds provided		$149,000
Applications of funds		
Purchase of equipment	$35,000	
Payment of cash dividends	28,000	
Purchase of land with bonds payable	16,000	
Retirement of preferred stock purchased with bonds payable	50,000	
Payment of mortgage with common capital stock	15,000	
Total funds applied		144,000
Increase in working capital		$ 5,000

AJAX CORPORATION

SCHEDULE OF CHANGES IN WORKING CAPITAL
FOR THE YEAR ENDED AUGUST 31, 19--

	End of Year	Beginning of Year	Working Capital Increase	Working Capital Decrease
Cash	$ 74,000	$ 80,000		$ 6,000
Receivables (Net)	122,000	166,000		44,000
Inventories	390,000	380,000	$10,000	
Accounts payable	89,000	134,000	45,000	
			$55,000	$50,000
Increase in working capital				5,000
			$55,000	$55,000

Transactions not involving cash appear as the last three items under both sources and applications on the Ajax funds statement. They did not affect current assets or current liabilities, but represent significant flows of other resources. They were of sufficient importance to require disclosure in the funds statement in order to make that statement acceptably complete. Had there been a wish to call attention more clearly to the items not affecting working capital, they could have been grouped in both sources and applications sections under a descriptive caption such as "transactions involving no cash."

THE CASH-FLOW STATEMENT

Many small enterprises operate on the cash basis, as indicated in Chapter 7. They measure their incomes and expenses, therefore, in terms of cash inflow and outflow, or cash receipts and disbursements. Large firms generally maintain their financial records on the accrual basis, which provides greater accuracy. A report based on the accrual method does not automatically furnish a record of cash received and expended. If such information is needed, it can be supplied in a *statement of cash flow,* prepared from the records, as will be explained later in this chapter.

CASH RECEIPTS AND DISBURSEMENTS STATEMENT

A *statement of cash received and disbursed* is, in effect, a rather detailed *cash-flow statement*. It bears some resemblance to a statement of changes in financial position, or funds statement, except that it will not report noncash transactions, such as an even exchange of one parcel of land for another.

An organization, such as a social club, which has no assets except cash in the treasurer's care, and no liabilities, will have no need for a balance sheet. Its sole financial statement, periodically, probably will be a *cash receipts and disbursements statement.* The statement will show cash on hand at the beginning of the period covered by the report, plus cash receipts, less cash disbursements, and the remaining balance at the end of the period, which represents cash on hand at that date. Purposes for which cash was received and paid out will be listed to the extent desired.

Only a relatively small number of organizations will find a cash statement to be sufficient for their financial reports, even when their operations are on a cash basis. If they have assets other than cash, and perhaps liabilities, the minimum requirement for their reports ordinarily will be a balance sheet, an income statement, and, probably, a funds statement.

An enterprise operating on the accrual basis will also find a statement of cash receipts and disbursements inadequate, requiring instead at least a balance sheet, an income statement, and, usually, a funds statement, to make a comprehensive and satisfactory report.

CASH EARNINGS

Financial reports occasionally contain comments about cash earnings, cash earnings per share, and cash flow, with or without accompanying explanatory schedules.

An income statement shows revenues, expenses, and net income, but it is not a statement of cash received and paid out. It can be converted to a cash basis, however, by adding back noncash expenses, such as depreciation, and adjusting for changes in current receivables and payables, prepaid and accrued items, and inventories.

Such adjustments for the Ajax Corporation income statement (page 160) will give the following results:

AJAX CORPORATION

CONVERSION OF INCOME STATEMENT TO CASH BASIS
FOR THE YEAR ENDED AUGUST 31, 19--

	Income Statement	Add (Subtract)	Cash Basis
Sales	$2,500,000		
Add decrease in accounts receivable		$ 44,000	$2,544,000
Cost of goods sold	1,490,000		
Add increase in inventory		$ 10,000	
Add decrease in accounts payable		45,000	1,545,000
Gross profit	$1,010,000		$ 999,000
Operating expenses	974,000		
Deduct depreciation		$(14,000)	960,000
Profit from operations	$ 36,000		$ 39,000
Profit from sale of land	13,000		13,000
Net profit	$ 49,000		$ 52,000

Net cash flow relating to revenues and expenses ordinarily is larger than net income. This is due, principally, to the omission of depreciation and other noncash items. For the Ajax Corporation, net cash flow was $52,000, but the net profit was $49,000. The $3,000 difference was not income, and any reference in the firm's financial report to the $52,000 "cash earnings" would cause some readers to be confused as to what the actual earnings were.

EARNINGS PER SHARE

Ajax Corporation's net income of $49,000 produced earnings per share of $11.95 for the 4,100 shares of capital stock outstanding. "Cash earnings" of $52,000 result in a figure of $12.68 per share. The cash earnings figure is misleading, however. It does not represent actual earnings.

As a matter of fact, Ajax did generate cash from operations amounting to $12.68 per share, compared with $11.95 per share net income. To a well-trained reader, the difference of $.73 gives some indication of the firm's ability to finance its operations. Nevertheless, there are valid objections to the inclusion of references to cash earnings in financial reports. Such references are likely to be misunderstood, even though a complete statement of changes in financial position accompanies the report, and the significance of the net income will be impaired.

Computation of earnings per share can be intricate when a corporation has several kinds of capital stock. For the Ajax Corporation, with only one class of stock outstanding at the close of the year, the $11.95 earnings per share are ascertained readily, and can be properly reported as such in its financial report for the year.

CASH-FLOW ANALYSIS

Net income reported on the accrual basis continues to be the best measure of a firm's operating performance. It does not, however, indicate the flow of cash generated by that performance. The flow of cash can be reported in a *cash-flow statement,* and management occasionally requests such a statement as an aid in reviewing the firm's financial policies.

When a cash flow statement is to be prepared, the income statement will be adjusted for various items. The Ajax net income of $36,000 from operations, for example, will be increased by the depreciation expense of $14,000, as it was for the funds statement, since depreciation expense did not affect working capital. Additional adjustments will be necessary to bring the accrual basis figures into harmony with the flow of cash. This will be accomplished by adjusting net income for increases and decreases in current receivables and payables, accrued and prepaid items, and inventories, in a manner somewhat similar to the adjustments made for conversion of the Ajax income statement to the cash basis.

Analysis of the Ajax balance sheet and supplemental information reveals the following:

1. Cash transactions to be included in cash-flow statement:
   a. Source of cash:
      Sale of land $18,000
   b. Application of cash:
      Purchase of equipment $35,000
      Payment of dividends 28,000
2. Noncash transactions to be excluded from cash-flow statement:
   a. Purchase of land for $16,000, for which bonds payable were issued
   b. Mortgage payable balance of $15,000 paid by issuance of capital stock
   c. Preferred stock retired, $50,000, acquired by issuance of bonds payable for that amount.

PREPARATION OF THE CASH-FLOW STATEMENT

A statement of cash flow sometimes can be prepared readily from the cash book of an organization, especially from a columnar cash book or when the number of transactions is small. It can also be constructed, often with less effort, with the help of a comparative balance sheet and supplemental information, as was the Ajax funds statement illustrated on page 155.

STATEMENT OF CASH FLOW

A cash-flow statement provides information about a firm's utilization of its cash resources. It can be helpful in the evaluation of financial policies and the current cash position, and also in the preparation of a cash budget. It is, therefore, of special interest to management, and of some interest to creditors and investors, present and prospective. The statement, however, is not generally believed to be essential for an understanding of a firm's financial activities, and while it will be prepared when requested for the use of management, it appears only occasionally in financial reports submitted to stockholders, bankers, and others.

A cash-flow statement for the Ajax Corporation follows, based on the comparative balance sheet and supplemental information already supplied.

AJAX CORPORATION
STATEMENT OF CASH FLOW
FOR THE YEAR ENDED AUGUST 31, 19--

Sources of cash:		
Operations:		
Net income, exclusive of $13,000 gain on sale of land		$36,000
Add: Depreciation of buildings and equipment	$14,000	
Decrease in current receivables	44,000	58,000
		$94,000
Deduct: Increase in inventories	$10,000	
Decrease in current payables	45,000	55,000
From operations		$39,000
Sale of land		18,000
Cash provided		$57,000
Applications of cash:		
Purchase of equipment	$35,000	
Payment of dividends	28,000	
Cash used		63,000
Decrease in cash		$ 6,000
Schedule of changes in cash:		
Cash balance, beginning of year		$80,000
Cash balance, end of year		74,000
Decrease in cash		$ 6,000

CHAPTER **17**

Industrial Accounting

A clear distinction can be made between a merchandising concern and a manufacturing enterprise. A merchandising enterprise purchases commodities and sells them in essentially the same form they had when acquired. A manufacturing enterprise, however, acquires commodities and applies labor to them, usually through the use of machinery, and produces a different commodity. This process creates many accounting problems, some of which will be discussed in this chapter.

PRODUCTION PROBLEMS

Large-Scale Production. Many manufacturing operations can be performed most effectively when they are conducted on a large scale. The very magnitude of such operations produces problems, many of which are of minor consequence in a small concern, and some of which are unknown to any but the largest concerns.

Some of these problems relate to the securing and proper training of personnel, the inability of managers to know all of the employees personally, the difficulty of obtaining competent superintendence, providing necessary capital, finding an adequate supply of raw materials, and planning a smooth flow of the product through the plant in the manufacturing process.

Industrial Combinations. Additional problems arise from the fact that many manufacturing concerns have been formed by combinations, and that production methods have been changed as a result of the combinations. Some of these problems are: record keeping for diversified properties, especially depreciation;

the flow of goods to the various plants, between the various plants, and from plants; personnel problems; and taxation.

Variety of Products. Frequently, one industrial concern manufactures a number of different products. This fact is important in all phases of accounting, especially in cost accounting. The task of the cost accountant would be relatively simple in an enterprise that manufactures only one product and has only one plant. As the number of products is increased, the task of the cost accountant becomes more complicated, and there is an increasing need for his services.

ELEMENTS OF MANUFACTURING COSTS

The three elements that enter the cost of manufacturing any product are raw materials, direct labor, and manufacturing expense, burden, or overhead. The sum of raw materials cost and direct labor cost is called *prime cost,* prime cost plus overhead is called *factory cost,* factory cost plus selling expenses equals *total cost,* and total cost plus profit or minus loss equals *selling price.*

ACCOUNTS IN A MANUFACTURING ENTERPRISE

In addition to many of the usual accounts found in mercantile and other enterprises, a typical manufacturing concern requires some accounts that are peculiar to its type of activities.

There are so many variations in the bookkeeping procedures of manufacturers, especially in relation to manufacturing costs, that only a general discussion of some typical procedures and accounts in a manufacturing enterprise is undertaken here.

1. *Inventories.* In a manufacturing business, there are three inventories, raw materials, goods in process, and finished goods, whereas a mercantile concern ordinarily has one merchandise inventory. Amounts of the three inventories can be ascertained, when desired, by physical count, and when perpetual inventory records are maintained, they disclose the inventory amounts continuously.

A *job order* cost accounting system, discussed later in

this chapter, maintains perpetual inventory records for each of the three types of inventory. This is an aid to management in obtaining cost data promptly instead of waiting for it until the end of the accounting period. The following three paragraphs summarize procedures for recording these inventories.

A controlling account, *raw materials,* is debited with the delivered costs of all purchases of raw materials and the amounts are entered on subsidiary *perpetual inventory cards.* Usually, there is a card for each kind of item listed in the raw materials inventory. Entries on the cards include both quantity and cost data, if desired. As materials are requisitioned for use in the manufacturing process, their costs are transferred to the goods in process account by debiting it and crediting raw materials. The transfers are also recorded on the inventory cards, which then show balances indicating the inventory of raw materials still on hand.

The *goods in process* account is charged with the cost of direct materials, direct labor, and the estimated amount of factory overhead expenses applicable to the goods in process of manufacture. A subsidiary *job cost ledger,* consisting of *job order sheets,* shows the accumulated costs of the individual jobs, or lots, in process. When production of a job is completed, the accumulated cost recorded on the related job order sheet is transferred by journal entry to the finished goods account and the job order sheet is removed to a file of completed sheets. The aggregate amount of the sheets remaining in the job cost ledger should agree with the balance in the goods in process account to show the cost of that inventory.

The *finished goods* account is debited when a completed production job is transferred to it from goods in process. The cost is also recorded in a subsidiary *finished goods ledger,* or *stock ledger,* which has an account for each type of finished product. When finished goods are sold, the usual entries recording the sale debit accounts receivable and credit sales with the selling price and also debit cost of goods sold and credit finished goods with the cost of the goods. This cost, as recorded on the appropriate account in the stock ledger, is entered on that account as a reduction of finished goods on hand. The sum of all of the adjusted accounts in the stock ledger should agree with the balance in the finished goods account in the general ledger to indicate the cost of the finished goods inventory on hand.

A *process cost* accounting system for a large and complex manufacturing enterprise usually requires perpetual inventory records, even when the manufactured products consist of relatively few kinds of items. Such records are somewhat similar to those used under a job order system. Many small concerns manufacture only a few products, using relatively simple processes. Their accounting records frequently can be maintained satisfactorily when inventory amounts are determined only periodically and such operating accounts as cost of goods manufactured are summarized at the end of each fiscal period. Unlike the perpetual inventory method, where purchases of raw materials are debited to the raw materials inventory account, the periodic inventory method charges such purchases to a raw materials purchases account, as indicated in the next paragraph.

2. *Purchases* and *transportation in.* All purchases of raw materials ordinarily are debited to a raw materials purchases account when a firm uses the periodic inventory method. At the close of a fiscal period, the raw materials purchases account is closed to the cost of goods manufactured account. A separate account, transportation in, frequently records freight and other delivery charges associated with purchases of raw materials.

3. *Purchase returns* and *purchase discounts.* The raw materials purchase returns and allowances account is credited for all returns and allowances in a manner similar to that followed by a mercantile enterprise. Purchase discounts usually are recorded in a separate account. At the close of the fiscal period, these accounts will be closed to the cost of goods manufactured account.

4. *Labor.* Wages paid for direct labor and for indirect labor

will be recorded in separate accounts. Direct labor will be charged for all labor applied directly to the products, while indirect labor will be charged for such things as supervision, maintenance, and factory clerical work which cannot be allocated directly to the product. The direct labor account is closed into the cost of goods manufactured account, and the indirect labor account into the overhead account, or burden account.

5. *Factory overhead,* or *burden.* In addition to indirect labor, the overhead, or burden, account will include such items as rent, heat, light, power, insurance, depreciation, and factory supplies. The burden account is closed into the cost of goods manufactured account. In a cost accounting system, the burden is sometimes distributed to the finished product upon the basis of direct labor, direct materials, machine hours, or some other appropriate method. When this is done, less than the total of the burden will be charged to the product at times, in which case the balance of the burden account will be underabsorbed burden. If more than the total of the burden is charged to the product, the credit balance of the burden account will be overabsorbed burden.

6. *Cost of goods manufactured.* A manufacturer's income statement sometimes includes an amount labeled cost of goods manufactured, which is supported by an attached schedule giving details about the composition of the amount. A summarizing ledger account, cost of goods manufactured, provides the data for this schedule.

Amounts to be recorded in the cost of goods manufactured account at the end of an accounting period include the opening and closing inventories of raw materials and goods in process, raw materials purchases, purchase returns and allowances, purchase discounts, transportation in, direct labor, and a number of factory overhead accounts. The final balance in the account is closed to cost of goods sold, or to the income summary account.

Instead of a cost of goods manufactured account, a firm may prefer a *manufacturing cost of goods sold* account, also called *cost of goods manufactured and sold.*

This account differs from the cost of goods manufactured account only in that it includes opening and closing finished goods inventories. An example of a statement of cost of goods manufactured and sold is given in Appendix A, on page 221.

Some accountants prefer the use of additional summarizing accounts, such as cost of goods manufactured, and a manufacturing summary account. Other accountants would limit the number of summarizing accounts to one income summary account, where feasible.

7. *Plant accounts.* An account may be maintained for each individual fixed asset. Frequently, such detailed records are kept in a separate subsidiary ledger called the plant ledger. Special forms of ledger sheets are available which provide supplementary information regarding the individual fixed asset, such as: date of acquisition, description, from whom acquired, cost, estimated life, estimated scrap or trade-in value, depreciation rate, disposal date, to whom transferred, amount received, and spaces for periodic depreciation charges.

8. *Intangibles.* A manufacturing concern frequently has accounts for such intangibles as goodwill, patents, trademarks, copyrights, franchises, formulas, leaseholds, and occasionally organization expense. The problem of placing an acceptable valuation upon such assets is sometimes difficult, although the general accounting rule is that if they are to be recognized as assets, they should be carried at cost less provision for the estimated amount of decrease in value since date of acquisition.

9. *Factory ledger account.* A company may decide to have the detailed accounts relating to manufacturing costs in an auxiliary self-balancing ledger, termed the *factory ledger*. In that event, a controlling account, the factory ledger account, is included in the general ledger. In the factory ledger, a general ledger account is the balancing account. The factory ledger account and the general ledger account are known as *interlocking*, or *reciprocal*, accounts. A debit balance in one, when the books are closed, must be the same amount as the credit balance in the other. They en-

able the factory ledger to be a self-balancing ledger. Most of the manufacturing accounts listed above probably will be included in such a factory ledger, and some of them, in turn, will be controlling accounts for other subsidiary ledgers.

STATEMENTS OF A MANUFACTURING BUSINESS

A work sheet is almost indispensable in preparation of financial statements of a manufacturing enterprise. Such a work sheet differs only slightly from that of a mercantile concern; the chief differences are that the work sheet of the manufacturing concern is likely to contain more accounts and have an additional pair of columns for the manufacturing costs or cost of goods manufactured. This entails no change in the principles involved in the use of the work sheet, but merely an extension of the principles already discussed.

Financial Statements. An income statement for a manufacturing concern differs from income statements previously discussed, not so much in the principal headings as in the detailed information included. Although little change need be made in the section headings, a section may contain either a greater number of items, or perhaps only one, while the details appear in a supplementary schedule. For instance, the cost of goods manufactured and sold section for a manufacturing concern contains much more information and more numerous accounts than does the cost of goods sold section of a mercantile enterprise. Included in this section are such items as additional inventories and the manufacturing expenses, mentioned above.

If this detailed information is not desired in the income statement, portions of it can be removed from that statement and shown in supplementary schedules. A schedule supporting the cost of goods manufactured and sold section may include all of the details that produce the total amount of that section, so that the income statement need show only the one amount and refer to the attached schedule. This is the plan followed in Appendix A, referred to previously.

If there is room on the income statement for some of the details of the cost of goods manufactured and sold, the supporting schedule can be limited to the cost of goods manufactured, or merely total manufacturing costs, or perhaps just the details of factory overhead costs.

Other sections of the income statement also require, at times, that supplementary schedules be used. Examples are schedules for selling expenses, general expenses, and nonoperating income and expenses.

Financial statements frequently appear in condensed form. They vary in the amount of detailed information shown as the purpose varies for which the statements are prepared. A statement for the use of the general public probably will be quite brief, statements prepared for the owners or stockholders will contain more details, and statements for the managers will give rather complete information.

Comparative statements are employed frequently, so that a statement for one fiscal period can be compared with similar financial statements for one or more other fiscal periods. Comparative statements include any type of financial statement or schedule, with or without comparative percentages, or ratios.

A balance sheet for a manufacturing concern differs from a balance sheet for a mercantile business in the presentation of inventories and frequently, in the predominance of fixed assets and the greater number of intangibles. A manufacturer will list the three inventories, raw materials, goods in process, and finished goods, whereas a retail store will have only one, its merchandise inventory. Sequence of items on the balance sheet tends to be the same, although some manufacturers prefer that the fixed assets be placed first, because of the relatively large amounts invested in them, followed by the current assets. If this arrangement is followed for the assets, a similar arrangement should be followed for the liabilities. This is in contrast to the current-to-fixed sequence commonly employed.

Supplementary Schedules. When detailed information is not desired on the financial statements, supplementary schedules are often employed, as suggested above, to show details omitted from the financial statements themselves. This is true of both the income statement and the balance sheet.

Balance sheet schedules include accounts receivable, accounts payable, investments, and fixed assets.

Sundry Reports. In addition to the financial statements and supplementary schedules, numerous other reports are employed by manufacturing enterprises. Most of them supply details needed by management. Some examples of this type of report are payroll reports, tax reports, production reports, receiving reports, shipping reports, and inventories.

COST ACCOUNTING

Cost accounting, as defined in Chapter 1, is the determination of the costs of doing business, especially unit costs of production and distribution. It is a specialized subject and is viewed by many accountants as a distinct field, separated from the work of the general accountant. To be most effective, however, it must be integrated with the general bookkeeping system in order to obtain the advantages of double-entry control.

Discussions of cost accounting tend to place major emphasis on the needs of manufacturing concerns. The benefits of a cost accounting system are also applicable, however, to other types of organization, to stores, to service enterprises such as hospitals and banks, and to governmental agencies.

Whereas the methods of accounting discussed in previous chapters compute total costs incurred by a firm during a period of time, cost accounting has the fundamental objective of determining unit costs of production or distribution of a given product, process, or service.

Cost accounting is relatively simple for a concern that produces only one product. Its costs can be computed in terms of units of production merely by dividing total costs for the period by the number of units produced during that period. However, a manufacturing enterprise producing more than one item faces far more difficult cost accounting problems. Its cost accounting system endeavors to allocate to each individual product its share of the costs. Costs so computed provide a basis for determining the proper selling price and the gross profit on the sale of each item.

A cost accounting system, properly planned and maintained, provides cost data, both actual and prospective, to assist management in the control of current operations, and in planning for the future.

Many methods of cost accounting are employed in industry. Probably no one plan could be adopted universally, because of the variety of problems encountered in business operations.

There are two principal systems of cost accounting, *job order cost*, or *specific order cost*, and *process cost*, or *continuous process cost*. Both systems, with variations, are widely used by concerns of all sizes. A company may require a job order cost system for some departments or products, and a process cost system for others.

Job Order Cost System. A job order cost accounting system provides a separate record of each job, or lot, or special order that an enterprise processes separately. A firm employing this system will maintain a *job order sheet, job cost sheet, job cost ticket,* or *production order,* for each job while it is being processed. Each job order sheet accumulates the costs incurred in the production of the specific job to which it relates. All of the job cost sheets that cover goods in process at any one time constitute the *job cost ledger,* which is a continuous record of the cost of the goods in process inventory.

This system is suitable for a business such as a building construction company or a printing plant, whose output is made to customers' specifications. Under such conditions, each job is unique and justifies a separate cost accumulation. This method also is useful when a company produces standard goods in batches as needed, rather than continuously, as in the shoe industry.

Continuous Process Cost System. A continuous process cost accounting system accumulates costs periodically for each department, or process, in a plant. This method is suitable for a concern that manufactures products by a continuous repetitive process without identification of individual lots or orders. Examples of such firms include producers of flour, cement, bricks, paint, electricity, and so on.

Process cost accounting differs from job cost accounting in the emphasis it places on time instead of individual lots produced.

It accumulates the costs of a department for a month, for instance, which can then be divided by the number of identical units of product produced during that month to obtain the average cost per unit.

Standard Costs. *Predetermined costs,* or *standard costs,* are estimates of what costs should be under given conditions. They should be based on careful study and analysis so that they will be reasonable and acceptable. They afford a means of comparing current operations with the planned results derived from such estimated costs, in order to judge the reasonableness of costs actually incurred. They also aid in budgeting future operations, predicting costs, quantities, and overall results, which will be compared later with actual results.

Standard costs, even when computed most carefully, seldom match exactly the costs actually incurred by operations. The differences, called *variances,* enable management to judge whether a department or an individual is performing as efficiently as was anticipated by the budget. When costs actually incurred are lower than the standard costs, the variance is favorable. An unfavorable variance results when actual costs are higher than standard costs. A variance of a significant amount justifies investigation by management to determine the cause or causes. Remedial measures can then be taken to correct an unfavorable situation and maintain a measure of control over costs.

CHAPTER 18

Departments, Branches, and Subsidiaries

DEPARTMENTS

A business enterprise generally sells more than one type of goods and services. In such cases, it is desirable, though not always feasible, to compute the incomes and expenses and the resulting profit separately for each commodity or service. A method of accounting which provides such separation is known as *departmental accounting*. Departmentalized accounting does not ordinarily involve a separation of the balance sheet items by departments, but does include a separation into departments of some of the income statement items. Operating incomes will be segregated by departments and a number of the expenses will be allocated directly to departments. This does not provide a complete income statement for each department, since some income and expense items cannot readily be broken down by departments and are therefore shown under general headings on the income statement.

Accounts for Departments. Ordinarily, no entirely new accounts will be required for departmentalized accounting. However, items of income and expense that are allocated to the departments will necessitate the subdivision of the accounts by departments. There probably will be a sales account for each department that makes sales. Such an account will have the general title *sales*, followed by its departmental designation, so that the labels of the sales accounts will be *sales: department A, sales: department B*, and so on.

Departmentalized Journals. The original record of transactions in departmentalized accounting should provide a method by which each transaction will be allocated to departments at the time it is recorded. In order to accomplish this, each income and expense item that would ordinarily be given a special column in a journal, will instead be given as many columns as there are departmental accounts for that item. The column headings should include the proper departmental designations, such as those suggested above for account titles. For instance, the purchase journal will need only one column for accounts payable, as this is a balance sheet item, but it will need as many columns for purchases as there are departments for which purchases are made. The same situation may readily be true of all other special journals.

Adjustments. Some transactions cannot be segregated by departments conveniently or accurately at the time they occur. Such transactions will be recorded originally as if there were no departments. If, at or before the close of the fiscal period, information becomes available that shows the proper distribution of such income or expenses, adjustments can be made at that time to record the allocations.

Financial Statements for a Departmentalized Enterprise. Ordinarily, financial reports to stockholders and the public are relatively brief and contain little, if any, information about individual departments. An alert management, however, will want extensive, detailed information at frequent intervals about departments under its control, giving special attention to any department that is not producing the results expected. Producing departments in a factory, having no income accounts, are judged on the basis of their costs, and the totals of all such costs find their way into the income statement prepared for the entire plant. Selling departments in a store can report their results with a separate income statement for each department, showing gross profit, and perhaps net profit, with the combined total of all such statements revealing the results of operations of the entire store in its income statement.

A departmentalized sales organization generally should be able to ascertain the gross profit for each department, as well as the total gross profit for the enterprise. Some concerns do not attempt to compute the net profit for each department if they find that such computations cannot be made accurately. In other enterprises, a net profit is computed for each department even if it necessitates the use of more or less arbitrary allocations. In all cases, as much information as possible should be shown for each department, in order to ascertain which departments are making profits, and which departments are operating at a loss. This information is important for management as an aid in formulating its policies.

BRANCHES

One phenomenon of the growth of business enterprises is the establishment of branches through which additional sales can be made and services rendered. Examples are the growth in the number of chain stores, branch banks, and branch manufacturing plants in recent years.

Care should be taken in the case of a mercantile concern that the term *agency* is not confused with the term *branch*.

One type of agency consists merely of a sales office which does not carry a full stock of merchandise, but takes orders which are delivered from the principal office, or home office. The customer is invoiced by the home office, which office also determines the credit to be extended and makes the collections.

Some offices, though not carrying a stock of merchandise, may invoice the customer, extend credit, and make the collections. Such an office has some of the characteristics of both an agency and a branch.

A branch usually maintains a sufficient inventory of merchandise to make deliveries to customers. In some branches, all of this merchandise is received from the general office. In others, a part of it will be purchased from independent vendors. A branch maintains its own credit department and makes the collections. Many variations are possible, and the accounting provisions will differ in some of the branches and agencies. Also, the accounting methods employed when there are a great many branches will differ somewhat from the methods followed when there are only a few branches and a smaller volume of business. The general principles involved are illustrated by the following discussion of a typical mercantile concern, assuming the existence of only a few branches.

Branch Accounting. The branch maintains a complete set of accounting records similar to those which would be used if the store were an independent enterprise. The principal distinction is that instead of proprietorship accounts, such as have been previously discussed, a home office account is used. This account represents the investment of the general, or central, office in the branch. The home office account in the branch ledger is reciprocal to the branch ledger account in the general ledger of the home office. The use of this reciprocal account makes the branch ledger a self-balancing ledger.

Use of Reciprocal Accounts. The controlling account, branch ledger, in the home office general ledger, is debited for the assets sent to the branch and for profit reported by the branch. It is credited for assets received from the branch and for losses reported by the branch. The reciprocal account, home office, in the branch ledger, is debited for assets sent to the home office and for losses incurred. It is credited for assets received from the home office and for profits. Since each of these accounts exhibits the same information, but on opposite sides, they are ordinarily termed *reciprocal* or *interlocking* accounts.

In addition to the set of accounting books provided for each branch, special records are often maintained in the home office. Special accounts are sometimes kept by the home office to record activities performed for the branches and not shown on the branch books in detail. Such activities can be recorded in summarized form on the branch books when periodic reports are received from the home office.

Financial Statements for an Enterprise with Branches. Independent financial statements sometimes are prepared for each branch and for the home office. An individual work sheet can be used as an accounting tool in the preparation of each of these statements, which is similar to the work sheet previously discussed. In addition, the home office will prepare a special combining work sheet from its books and branch reports. In the use of this work sheet, care should be taken to provide for the elimination of intracompany transactions. From such special work sheet, the formal combined income statement and balance sheet will be prepared.

In addition to the financial statements, various operating reports are usually prepared by each branch and by the home office. These reports are for the use of the management, according to its individual needs. Therefore, their extent, scope, and form will vary greatly among enterprises.

TRENDS TOWARD BUSINESS COMBINATIONS

One phenomenon of the business world, previously mentioned, is the growth of large-scale business enterprises. Large-scale enterprises frequently arise from combinations of previously existing business units. Such combinations are effected by *mergers, consolidations,* and the creation of *holding companies.*

Emphasis in recent years has been shifting from the legal form of the business combination to distinctions between a *new ownership* and *continuance of the former ownership.* New ownership results from a purchase, or acquisition, while retention of substantially all of the former ownership of the participating corporations signifies a pooling of interests.

TYPES OF BUSINESS COMBINATIONS

Merger. A *merger* is a business combination in which the acquiring company retains its name, whereas the acquired companies lose their identities. Such a merger usually means that the purchasing company acquires the assets of the other enterprises and assumes their liabilities. Payment for the acquired companies is made in various forms, including cash, or other assets, or stock in the purchasing corporation.

Consolidation. A *consolidation* is a business combination in which a new corporation is created which acquires the assets and assumes the liabilities of two or more previously existing companies. In a consolidation, all the combined companies lose their identities. Payment for the acquired companies is made in cash, or other assets, or in stock of the new corporation.

Holding Company. A *holding company* is a corporation whose principal function is to own at least a controlling amount of the capital stock outstanding of one or more other corporations, known as subsidiaries. A *parent company* differs from a holding company only in the fact that it is an operating company. The distinction is not always easily made, however, since some holding companies engage in operations in one or two departments. When more than 50 per cent of the outstanding capital stock is owned by another corporation, obviously that is a sufficient amount to control the subsidiary corporation. Quite frequently, much less than 50 per cent of the stock will be a sufficient amount to secure control. This situation is due to such factors as the wide spread of stock ownership, the antipathy of small stockholders to voting, the lack of organization of minority stockholders, and the willingness of small stockholders to vote with an organized group.

No difficulty of an unusual nature is encountered in preparing the financial statements for corporations combined through either a merger or a consolidation. In such cases, there need be only one set of books, and the methods of preparing financial statements previously discussed can be employed readily. However, when a combination has been brought about through the holding company device, the preparation of useful financial statements is more difficult. For instance, both the holding company and the subsidiary companies retain their separate legal existences, yet the companies may be so interrelated that they comprise one financial entity. In the preparation of informative reports for a holding company, its financial statements must be combined with the financial statements of the subsidiary companies. Such a combination results in a consolidated balance sheet and a consolidated income statement.

Pooling of Interests. Many business combinations result from an exchange of stock instead of a purchase. When such an exchange of stock provides that substantially all of the ownership in the participating corporations is continued in the new enterprise, it is called a *pooling of interests.*

Two or more corporations which pool their interests combine their operations in the new organization. They retain their former ownership, and they use their equipment, which has not been changed by the pooling arrangement. Accounting records for the new entity include transfer of this equipment from the participating companies at book value without adjustment.

Pooling of interests differs from a *purchase,* or *acquisition,* as previously indicated, by continuing the former ownership, whereas an acquisition results in new ownership of the constituent companies. Accounting for an acquisition often involves a new valuation for balance sheet items of the acquired companies and the inclusion of goodwill.

CONSOLIDATED STATEMENTS

Consolidated financial statements are prepared by summarizing the statements of the affiliated companies and then eliminating the intercompany transactions. Obviously, the balance sheets should be for the same date, and the income statements should include operations for the same period of time.

The Investment Account. A holding company's investment account is replaced on the consolidated balance sheet by the assets and liabilities of the subsidiary companies. Some holding companies operate on a limited scale, but in any case the investment account of a holding company does not provide a meaningful figure for use on the balance sheet when it includes stock of subsidiary corporations. In the preparation of consolidated statements, a special work sheet is generally used.

Intercompany Eliminations. Eliminations of intercompany accounts are essential to the preparation of consolidated statements. They are made, usually, in two columns reserved for intercompany eliminations on the work sheet of the parent company. Four principal groups of intercompany eliminations are as follows:

1. *Intercompany receivables and payables.* Advances, accounts receivable, notes receivable, and bonds are included in these eliminations when they are a part of transactions among affiliated companies.

2. *Intercompany profits in inventories.* These profits should not be included in the financial statements. Profits should be eliminated which arise from intercompany transactions

involving merchandise still on hand at the close of the fiscal period.

3. *Investments in subsidiaries.* Such investments should not be shown on the consolidated balance sheet, although investments in corporations may be included if they are not sufficiently large to bring about control.

4. *Intercompany income and expense items,* including sales and purchases and intercompany dividends, should be eliminated from the consolidated income statement since they are transactions among parts of a financial entity.

Periodic Financial Statements. A consolidated income statement and a consolidated balance sheet are prepared as if the affiliated companies were a single unit. If the holding company owns 100 per cent of the outstanding capital stock of the subsidiary companies, preparation of the financial statements is relatively easy. Frequently, however, the amount of stock owned is less than 100 per cent, making the procedure for preparation of the financial statement more complicated if an accurate and true picture of the affiliated group is to be shown. Particularly important is the showing of the status of minority stockholders within the group. Usually, the holdings of minority stockholders are shown as a part of proprietorship on the consolidated balance sheet, but sometimes they are listed as liabilities.

CHAPTER **19**

Advanced Discussion of Accounts

INVESTMENTS

Companies frequently own stocks and bonds of other companies, and bonds of the United States government and other governmental units. Sometimes, readily saleable stocks and bonds are held as a liquid investment. In such cases, the investments are intended to supplement the cash and provide income producing assets in place of cash not needed for day-to-day transactions. Investments so held are usually shown on the balance sheet along with the other current assets, although some accountants prefer to place them in a separate section between current assets and fixed assets.

Stocks and bonds held for purposes of control with the intention of retaining them until maturity, or at least for an extended period of time, can properly be shown on the balance sheet either with the fixed assets or in a separate section between current assets and fixed assets. Stocks and bonds shown as investments may be retained by the company as a matter of business policy; some investments are held for purposes of control, and others are held for the purpose of maintaining satisfactory business relationships with customers.

In general, the purpose for which investments are held determines their position on the balance sheet, temporary investments being treated as current assets, and permanent investments as other assets, except that both kinds are at times shown in a separate investments section between current assets and fixed assets.

180

DISCOUNTS

Cash Discounts. On wholesale transactions, a customer is frequently permitted to pay less than the amount of the invoice if payment is made within a stated limited period. Such a deduction is referred to as a cash discount. For example, when the terms of a sale are "2/10, n/30," the customer deducts 2 per cent if he pays the invoice within 10 days of its date, but, if he delays payment, the net or entire amount will be due in 30 days. An enterprise treats cash discounts taken by customers as *sales discounts,* and cash discounts allowed by creditors as *purchase discounts.*

Sales discounts may appear on the income statement in the sales, the operating expenses, or the nonoperating expenses sections. If sales discounts are in the sales section, they are a deduction from gross sales. If they are in the operating expenses section, they are either a selling expense or a general and administrative expense. If they are in the nonoperating expenses section, they are a nonoperating expense.

Purchase discounts are often shown on the income statement in the cost of goods sold section as a deduction from purchases. Sometimes, they are placed in the general and administrative expenses division of the operating expenses section as a financial management income, offsetting financial management expenses. They are also included in the nonoperating income and expenses section at times as a nonoperating income.

While there is some difference of opinion as to the proper place for sales discounts and purchase discounts on the income statement, a consistent policy should be followed by a business concern.

Purchase Discounts Not Taken. An enterprise can save a substantial amount by paying for its purchases promptly to obtain the benefit of cash discounts. Payment for a $100 purchase at the end of 10 days, for example, when the terms are 2/10, n/30, requires only $98, the $2 saving being the result of paying 20 days before the total amount would be due. A saving of 2% in 20 days is equivalent to 36% a year. Such savings are recorded, generally, in a purchase discount account, to be treated as a deduction from purchases, or as an income item.

When purchase discounts are recorded, purchases account generally is debited and accounts payable credited for the full amount of each purchase. Then, if a discount is taken at the time of payment, the full purchase price is debited to accounts payable to cancel the liability, cash is credited for the smaller amount paid, and purchase discounts is credited for the difference. If payment is too late to obtain the discount, the entire purchase price is payable and will be debited to accounts payable and credited to cash. With this method, the books will show the total amount of purchase discounts taken during the accounting period, but will not disclose discounts forfeited through failure to pay invoices within the discount period.

An alternative method of handling purchase discounts provides that, instead of recording such discounts as income, the loss resulting from failure to take them is listed as an expense. When this method is followed, a purchase subject to a cash discount is recorded at its net amount, that is, the full purchase price less the cash discount. Purchases account is debited and accounts payable credited for the net amount, which is the amount payable to the vendor if the bill is paid within the discount period. If so paid, that amount is debited to accounts payable and credited to cash. If payment is delayed beyond the discount period, the full amount of the invoice must be paid, requiring a debit to accounts payable for the net amount previously credited there, a debit to an account such as discounts lost for the amount of discount not taken, and a credit to cash for the full amount paid. The discounts lost account thus measures the cost of failures to pay for purchases within the discount periods provided. With this method, purchases appear on the income statement at net cost, that is, full purchase price less all purchase discounts, whether taken or not, and discounts lost are an additional cost or expense.

Trade Discounts. A rather common business procedure is the allowance of a deduction from the catalogue price, or list price, of merchandise to determine the invoice price without reference to the date of payment. Such an allowance is ordinarily termed a *trade discount* and will include allowances made for various reasons. All customers may be given a trade discount, either to conceal the actual price from persons who might see the catalogue, or to avoid rewriting the catalogue. The trade discount can be changed when the price level changes and no new catalogue need be issued. Individual customers can be favored through the granting of trade discounts not given to all customers. This is sometimes done to meet competition, to grant lower prices to affiliated companies, or to provide secret rebates. Trade discounts are frequently allowed on the basis of the quantity of merchandise purchased.

Discount on Notes. Interest collected in advance by banks or others on loans to customers is known as *discount*. The portion of discount on notes payable that is applicable to the current fiscal period will be shown on the income statement as interest expense. If part of the discount is not consumed at the close of the fiscal period, such part will ordinarily be shown on the balance sheet as prepaid interest expense, a deferred charge.

The portion of discount on notes receivable earned during the accounting period is interest income. The unearned portion is interest received in advance, ordinarily a deferred credit to income.

Discount on Bonds. Bonds may be sold for less than face value. This gives rise to a discount on bonds, which was mentioned in Chapter 15. The issuing corporation treats this as discount on bonds payable, which is a deferred charge to interest expense. The investor purchasing bonds for less than the face value can properly record the discount as a discount on bonds receivable, which is a deferred credit to income.

Discount on Capital Stock. When stock is issued for less than its par value, it is said to be issued at a discount, as was indicated in Chapter 14. When stock is originally issued at a discount, the discount should be shown on the balance sheet as a deduction from the par value of the stock. When a corporation reacquires its own stock, such stock is known as treasury stock. If treasury stock is acquired for less than the par value, the difference between the amount paid and par value is a discount on treasury stock. If the stock was debited to an account, treasury stock, at cost when purchased, and it is not to be reissued, an acceptable entry to cancel it will debit the original capital stock account for the amount recorded there when it was first issued, presumably at par, credit treasury stock account for the purchase price, and credit the difference to a proprietorship account such as paid-in capital from treasury stock transactions.

If the stock is reissued, the above canceling entry will not be needed, but instead, an asset account (cash, if sold for cash) will be debited, treasury stock account credited for the purchase price there recorded, and paid-in capital from treasury stock transactions account debited or credited for the difference.

CAPITAL AND REVENUE EXPENDITURES

An expenditure is the payment of money or services or the incurring of debts for any asset or expense. Expenditures are customarily divided into two groups, *capital expenditures* and *revenue expenditures.*

A capital expenditure is one that increases the value at which a fixed, or capital, asset may properly be carried on the books. Capital expenditures sometimes are termed charges to capital, capital charges, or asset expenditures.

A revenue expenditure is one that constitutes a proper deduction from income, or revenue. It is an expense. Revenue expenditures are sometimes termed charges to revenue, charges against revenue, revenue charges, charges to operations, or expense expenditures.

When distinguishing between capital and revenue expenditures, the term *capitalizing* appears frequently. Capitalizing is the charging of an expenditure to an asset account.

Proper distinction must be made between capital expenditures and revenue expenditures. If this is not done, the periodic financial statements will be incorrect. If a revenue expenditure is recorded improperly as a capital expenditure, expense will be understated, and net profit, assets, and proprietorship will be overstated. If a capital expenditure is improperly shown as a revenue expenditure, the opposite will be true; expense will be overstated, and net profit, assets, and proprietorship will be understated.

CAPITAL GAINS AND LOSSES

Income tax laws define certain types of assets as *capital assets* and accord special tax treatment to gains or losses resulting from sales or exchanges of such assets. When disposed of before they have been held six months, the gain or loss is a *short-term capital gain* or a *short-term capital loss*. If held for six months or more, the gain or loss is a *long-term capital gain* or a *long-term capital loss*. Capital assets include almost everything a taxpayer owns except property used in a trade or business, and under restricted conditions, some business assets are also treated as capital assets. Capital gains and losses ordinarily will appear on the income statement as nonoperating items.

SALES

Sales, as previously discussed, have included principally the transfer of merchandise for cash or on credit. These two types of sales are the ones generally encountered in sales transactions. There are other common types of sales, however, some of which are: C.O.D. sales, approval sales, installment sales, sales for future delivery, and sales of consigned goods.

Cash Sales. A sale for which the vendor receives the full amount of the sale contract price in cash at the time the sale is consummated is known as a cash sale.

Sales on Credit. Sales on credit are sales of assets, or of services, for which payment will be made at some later date.

C.O.D. Sales. The term C.O.D. is merely an abbreviation for cash, or collect, on delivery. This kind of sale is similar to the cash sale, the difference being that cash is received at the time delivery is made. When delivery is made by the vendor, title passes at time of delivery. When delivery is made by a common carrier, title usually passes at the time goods are turned over to the carrier, although possession may not be taken until payment is made.

Approval Sales. When goods are delivered to a customer for his approval, a memorandum record should be made, but title has not passed and a sale should not be recorded until the customer has indicated that he will retain the goods.

Installment Sales. This type of sale on credit is one in which the vendor usually receives part of the price of the goods at the time the sale is made, and the purchaser agrees to pay the balance at more or less regular intervals over a period of time. There are two principal types of installment sales, one in which title passes at the time of the sale, subject to a chattel mortgage held by the seller, and another in which title does not pass to the purchaser until the merchandise is paid for in full. In an installment sale, the seller records his profit as earned: (1) at the time the sale is made, (2) in proportion to the installments received, or (3) after all costs have been recovered.

Ordinarily, accountants prefer to treat the profit from installment sales as realized at the time of sale, with appropriate provision for uncollectible accounts. However, in exceptional cases, where there is no reasonable basis for estimating the degree of cellectibility, the profit may be recorded either in proportion to the installments received, or after all costs have been recovered.

Sales for Future Delivery. When a sale is made and the merchandise is to be delivered at some future date, profits frequently are not recorded until the time of delivery.

Sales of Consigned Goods. A firm that sells at wholesale sometimes arranges with a retail dealer to accept some of its merchandise on consignment. The wholesaler, who is the *consignor,* delivers the goods to the retailer, who is the *consignee,* but the title remains with the consignor until final disposition of the goods. The consignee sells the consigned goods for the account of the consignor. Such transactions, which in reality are bailments, should be recorded in a separate account, when feasible, to distinguish them from sales of the company's own merchandise. The consigned goods, being the property of the consignor, must be included in the inventory of the consignor and carefully excluded from the inventory of the consignee.

ACCOUNTING FOR SALES

Procedures vary in accounting for sales. They generally involve special journals, ledgers, and registers, and some degree of mechanized accounting, and, in large organizations, probably punched cards and electronic computers. Although variations in accounting for sales are many, some general principles can be listed. For a cash sale, the entry consists of a debit to cash and a credit to sales. For a credit sale, the entry consists of a debit to the individual customer's account, and usually a debit to the accounts receivable controlling account, and a credit to sales. For a C.O.D. sale, a debit may be made to a C.O.D. account and to the accounts receivable controlling account, and a credit to sales. If goods are returned because payment is not received, an entry is made to debit sales, and credit the C.O.D. account and the accounts receivable controlling account. For installment sales, there are several ways in which the entries are made, some differences being due to the various times in which profits on installment sales are computed. For sales for future delivery, only a memorandum record is necessary prior to delivery of the merchandise. Upon delivery, the entry will be made in accordance with the way in which payment is received. In accounting for sales of consigned goods, it is important that the entries made will enable both the consignor and consignee to have a complete picture of the transactions.

CHAPTER 20

Accounting and Management

GROUPS FOR WHOM STATEMENTS ARE PREPARED

Diverse groups interested in a business enterprise do not have precisely the same viewpoint, and therefore the financial statements prepared especially for them will vary in the type and extent of details presented.

1. *Management* is interested in the financial statements, especially a detailed profit and loss statement, in order to secure information needed for efficient operation of the enterprise. The statements should be shown in sufficient detail to enable the managers, through analysis and interpretation, to evaluate past operations and formulate future policies.

2. *Owners* sometimes are managers of small business enterprises, but in corporations, especially large ones, owners and managers usually are different individuals. Financial statements prepared for the use of the owners should enable them to judge the efficiency of the management, and evaluate the progress being made by the firm.

3. *Prospective owners* may wish to see and evaluate a firm's financial statements before investing in it.

4. *Creditors* are interested in statements which will indicate the ability of the enterprise to meet its obligations at maturity. Short-term creditors are interested in the liquidity of the enterprise, whereas long-term creditors are interested in its ability to make interest payments, as well as its ability to meet obligations in the more distant future. This is true of both present and prospective creditors.

5. *Employees* have been given statements, particularly in recent years, which present a readily understandable picture of the operations and condition of the enterprise, and its relationship to the employees. While such statements are not used by all businesses, they are a means of keeping the employees informed and interested in the business. Some employees are also stockholders. This gives them a dual interest in the enterprise.

6. *Governmental agencies* frequently require financial statements for such purposes as taxation and control. The requirements of the Securities and Exchange Commission are an example. The reports and returns so required appear in many forms to which the enterprise must conform.

7. The *public* is interested in the financial statements that indicate the security and stability of such enterprises as banks, insurance companies, and public utilities. The financial statements of a public utility company may assist the public in judging correctness of the rates charged. Financial reports of governmental units should be made available to the public.

ANALYSIS AND INTERPRETATION OF FINANCIAL STATEMENTS

The accounting department prepares analyses and interpretations of financial statements as required by the management. These statements can include information desired by all of the groups mentioned above. The accounting records furnish much of the information upon which the analyses are based. Frequently, no interpretation of the statements is attempted by the accounting department, but it is left to the judgment of those who use the statements. In the preparation of an analysis, various devices are used, several of which are indicated in the following paragraphs.

Percentages. *Percentages* are helpful in the analysis of both balance sheets and income statements. They are employed on the balance sheet so that each percentage listed shows the proportion of a specific asset, or group of assets, to a larger group, or to total assets. The same procedure is followed in connection with both the liabilities and proprietorship. On the income statement, each percentage listed shows the proportion of one item, or group of items, to a larger group, or to some base figure such as sales.

Ratios. A *ratio* indicates the relationship of one number to another. In the analysis of balance sheets and income statements, a number of ratios are employed, some of which have considerable significance if properly interpreted. Valuable information about trends in an enterprise can be obtained by comparing similar ratios on a series of balance sheets or income statements. In discussing a ratio, care should be taken to state it correctly. It is computed by dividing the first named item by the second. Following are some of the typical financial statement ratios:

1. Current assets to current liabilities (the current ratio). The excess of current assets over current liabilities (net current assets) is called *working capital*. Some accountants prefer to call the net current assets *net working capital.*
2. The total of cash, receivables, and marketable securities to current liabilities (the acid test ratio)
3. Notes receivable to accounts receivable
4. Merchandise inventories to current assets
5. Current assets to total assets
6. Plant and equipment to fixed liabilities
7. Fixed assets to total assets
8. Fixed assets to fixed liabilities
9. Notes payable to accounts payable
10. Total liabilities to total assets
11. Total liabilities to proprietorship
12. Capital stock to fixed assets
13. Retained earnings to total proprietorship
14. Proprietorship to fixed assets
15. Proprietorship to total assets
16. Net profit to net sales
17. Cost of goods sold to average merchandise inventory (the merchandise turnover)
18. Net sales to receivables
19. Net sales to fixed assets
20. Net sales to proprietorship

21. Net profit to proprietorship
22. Net profit to capital stock
23. Net profit less dividends on preferred stock to common capital stock
24. Net profit to total assets.

Comparative and Cumulative Statements. These statements are used frequently in analyses. Both the balance sheet and the income statement can be prepared in either comparative or cumulative form. *Comparative statements* provide a method of comparing the financial statements of one period with similar statements of one or more preceding periods. This is accomplished by showing in one column the figures for the current period, while in one or more other columns will be shown the figures with which comparison is to be made. A separate column is sometimes used to show the amount of increase or decrease, and yet another column to show the percentage increase or decrease.

Cumulative statements usually are interim statements prepared at intervals during a fiscal year. Each statement contains a column to show the figures for the current part of the year, such as one month, and another column to show the cumulative figures for the year to date.

A combination may be used which provides both comparative and cumulative information. In this variation one column is used for the current figures, another column for figures for the same period last year, a third column for the cumulative total to date for this fiscal year, and a fourth column for the cumulative total to this same date for the preceding fiscal year.

Need for Supplementary Statements. *Supplementary statements,* or *supplementary schedules,* are prepared particularly for the use of the management. Such statements ordinarily include information in greater detail than is desired on the formal financial statements. Examples are the schedules relating to the balance sheet. A schedule, or abstract, of accounts receivable and of accounts payable will list the individual accounts remaining on the books at the close of the fiscal period, together with the amounts involved. The totals of such lists will be the same as the amounts shown for accounts receivable and accounts payable on the balance sheet. Other supporting schedules show detailed information concerning such balance sheet items as notes receivable, notes payable, cash, machinery, and buildings.

In addition to a schedule of bank balances which comprise the cash total, a detailed schedule may provide an analysis and classification of the receipts and disbursements of cash.

An analysis of sales is frequently prepared to provide a breakdown of the sales figure in various ways. One method shows separately the amounts of sales for cash and on credit. Another method shows an analysis of sales on the basis of the type of commodity sold. Another lists sales by departments. A fourth method shows the geographical distribution of sales. Other analyses will be prepared to provide additional supplementary information as desired by management.

Frequently, it is essential that supplementary statements be prepared promptly if the management is to use them in policy determination. The work sheet is an almost indispensable aid in the rapid preparation of financial statements, both formal and supplementary, especially for a large organization.

INTERNAL CONTROL

A system of *internal control,* or *internal checks,* comprises all of the measures and methods used by an organization for the purpose of: (1) protecting its resources, (2) securing accuracy in all of its operating data, (3) promoting efficiency, and (4) encouraging adherence to prescribed company policies.

A basic requirement of internal control is that the work of each person is verified automatically, without duplication of effort, by another person. The result of this interrelationship of the work of various employees is that: (1) errors, when they do occur, are usually detected and corrected promptly, and (2) fraud is almost impossible to conceal without collusion.

Good management wants assurance that its internal control system is operating as planned, in order to have the benefits that it can provide. The independent auditor, who examines the firm's financial records, is deeply concerned about the effectiveness of the internal control system and the extent to which he can rely on its dependability. The internal auditor, a member of the firm's own staff, is interested likewise as he examines various aspects of the firm's operations and the effectiveness with which the internal control system works.

BUDGETING

Budgeting provides a compelling reason for the analysis of a firm's financial statements by its management. A budget is a systematic forecast of business operations in financial terms. Such a forecast should be based upon an adequate knowledge of the firm's past operations, which is strengthened by a thorough analysis of its financial statements.

Budgeting is used not only by business enterprises established to earn a profit, but also by nonprofit organizations such as churches and governmental units. Increased use of budgetary accounting in recent years has provided management with an important tool for the efficient operation of an enterprise.

Procedures in budgetary accounting are complex, and many variations occur. Nevertheless, some basic principles are observable. A budget may be prepared for each department in an enterprise, and then a combined budget established for the entire organization. Preparation of the budget usually is under the control of an administrative officer, who works with the departments in the establishment of departmental budgets in keeping with the desired budget for the entire organization. A budget for a large enterprise involves preparation in advance of estimated balance sheets and income statements. Periodically, the estimated financial statements should be compared with the statements reporting results of actual operations, in order to assist the management in the formation and revision of business policies.

INSOLVENCY

When an enterprise is unable to meet its obligations, it is insolvent. It is possible for an insolvent enterprise to continue to operate.

Actions necessary to have a court declare an insolvent enterprise bankrupt can be voluntary or by action of the creditors. Liquidation of a bankrupt concern must proceed under strict court supervision.

A *statement of affairs* is an accounting statement somewhat similar to a balance sheet, prepared to indicate what the creditors can expect to receive from the liquidation of the business. This statement differs from the balance sheet particularly in the method of valuing the items and in the order of their presentation. Assets are usually classified as those assets which are fully pledged, partly pledged, and unpledged. Liabilities are classified as those liabilities which are preferred, fully secured, partly secured, unsecured, and contingent. A statement of affairs ordinarily shows not only the book value of the assets, but also the amount expected to be realized from the assets.

A statement of affairs is customarily accompanied by a *deficiency account,* which is supplementary and indicates how the deficiency shown on the statement of affairs arises.

VOCATIONAL AND PROFESSIONAL ASPECTS

Accounting Work Classified. Those who engage in accounting activity can be classified as follows: bookkeeper, accountant, cost accountant, chief accountant, auditor, controller, public accountant, and certified public accountant.

Representative Accounting Organizations. Probably, the best known of the numerous accounting organizations in the United States are the American Institute of Certified Public Accountants (AICPA); state societies of certified public accountants; American Accounting Association (AAA); National Association of Accountants (NAA), formerly named National Association of Cost Accountants; The Institute of Internal Auditors (IIA); Financial Executives Institute (FEI); American Woman's Society of Certified Public Accountants (AWSCPA); American Society of Women Accountants (ASWA); and Federal Government Accountants Association (FGAA).

Accounting Literature. Current accounting literature published by the organizations named above includes the following journals: *The Journal of Accountancy,* published monthly by AICPA;

The Accounting Review, published quarterly by AAA; *Management Accounting,* published monthly by NAA; *The Internal Auditor,* published monthly by IIA; *Financial Executive,* published monthly by FEI; *The Woman CPA,* published bi-monthly by AWSCPA and ASWA; and *The Federal Accountant,* published quarterly by FGAA. A digest of numerous accounting articles from magazines throughout the world is published privately in the quarterly magazine *The Accountants Digest.*

CHAPTER 21

Mechanized Accounting

MACHINE APPLICATIONS IN ACCOUNTING

Mechanical Aids. Many of the accounting procedures discussed in previous chapters are carried on with the help of mechanical equipment. But mechanical assistance is not always necessary. Given sufficient time, one or more persons can maintain the financial records of a business manually, writing with pen and ink in the journals and ledgers, and preparing financial reports without the help of any machines. Such bookkeeping produces satisfactory records for many small concerns.

Manual methods are somewhat slow, however, and most businesses would not be able to accumulate and process their financial data efficiently without the help of mechanical devices. Machines have been developed that produce the desired accounting records with greater speed and accuracy than is possible with hand methods. Machine methods can be more economical, also, if the volume of transactions to be recorded is sufficiently large.

Even some of the smallest businesses, as well as all of the large ones, employ various mechanical aids to assist the recording process.

Types of Mechanical Equipment. Machines most often used by firms of all sizes to help maintain their financial records are cash registers, typewriters, and adding and calculating machines.

Concerns with a large volume of transactions to record turn for help to more sophisticated, more expensive, mechanical equipment, such as bookkeeping machines that combine the functions of a typewriter and an adding machine, punched card equipment, and electronic computers.

Other machines, which serve in a supplementary capacity, include the check writer, check cutter and stacker, check protecting device, duplicator, addresser, time recorder, coin sorter, coin counter, money changer, teletypewriter, and others.

Advantages of Machine Operation. While advantages gained by the use of mechanical accounting equipment vary, the following are commonly recognized:

1. Speed in operation and in preparation of reports
2. Accuracy
3. Neatness
4. More details available than with hand-written records
5. Balances and other information readily and continuously available.

The promptness with which accounting records produced by machines can supply a wide range of current and other information is one important factor in a large enterprise in assisting management to control present operations and to plan for the future. Management executives, faced with the need for making a decision promptly, frequently ask for information that would be impossible to supply without specialized data processing equipment.

CHARACTERISTICS OF MECHANIZED ACCOUNTING

Program. A mechanical device such as an electronic computer is capable of performing practically all of the functions of financial record keeping, but, being only a machine, it must be guided every step of the way by a detailed set of instructions, called a *program.*

Such a program generally is written in a *computer language,* or *programming language.* Three widely used computer languages are known as FORTRAN (FORmula TRANslation), COBOL (COmmon Business Oriented Language), and BASIC.

These languages are used for a variety of computers with differing technical requirements for programs. A computer will accept any one of them and convert the programming language by means of a *compiler* into its own particular *machine language.*

A program usually is a lengthy and costly document, containing a multitude of detailed step-by-step instructions which must be carefully designed and assembled in the proper order by skilled programmers. Programs for many data processing operations are available from the libraries of the manufacturers of computers, and sometimes with only minor changes they can be adapted to the specific needs of a company.

If a program directing a machine how to record accounting data is to operate effectively, it must apply to each step the same accounting principles that govern accounting records written by hand, which involve debits and credits, journals and ledgers, controlling and subsidiary accounts, and financial reports and other documents to be derived from the accounts. A program must be free from error as well, since the machine follows exactly the instructions given in the program; if the instructions are incorrect, the answers obtained by the machine will be incorrect.

Machine-made accounting records frequently differ in appearance from the hand-written kinds, but the difference will be in appearance only if they are based on the same underlying principles.

Decisions. A computer can make *decisions* in a limited way, but not in the sense of expressing judgment. Regardless of its complexity, it cannot think; it has no will of its own; but it can choose among alternatives when specifically directed by a program. Two examples will illustrate this ability: (1) a computer can reject, or set aside for special consideration, a sales order from a customer that would make the unpaid amount of his account exceed a predetermined maximum credit limit, and (2) a computer can be programmed to control inventory quantities by preparing automatically a purchase order or other memorandum when a commodity listed on the perpetual inventory records reaches a designated minimum amount. The order for the replenishment will state the quantity which has been selected as the most economical to buy or produce.

Input. Every data processing system consists of three major parts: (1) input, (2) processing, and (3) output.

Input is the information introduced into the system. Any acceptable means for transmitting this information to the processing equipment is known as an *input device*. With mechanized accounting, the input device furnishes a way to communicate in code with the machines, providing them with information and telling them what to do with it.

There are various kinds of input devices, including punched cards, punched paper tape, magnetized tape, electric typewriters with punched tape connected with a computer in a distant city, special telephones capable of communicating in a limited fashion with a computer, marks on paper with a special pencil as in some types of examinations, and magnetic ink characters on paper as on bank checks.

Punched cards provide a flexible record, since the many kinds of information punched into them can be assembled in any desired order by sorting and resorting the cards, and new cards can be added and old ones withdrawn readily or punched to record additional information. For example, the cards can speedily supply such data as sales by departments, by salesmen, by geographic areas, by classes of merchandise, by sizes and colors, and so on. Punched cards are discussed again later in this chapter.

Punched paper tape delivers its information to a computer at higher speeds than is possible with punched cards, and it is less bulky than cards, but it does not permit rearrangement of the data it carries or insertion of additional information after the tape has been punched. It can be punched by typewriters, adding machines, or cash registers as they record business transactions. It is useful in the transmission of telegrams and in forwarding business data among offices by teletype or by mail.

Magnetic tape consists of plastic tape coated with ferric oxide on which data can be placed by magnetizing small spots on it. Magnetic tape requires less storage space than punched paper tape, and corrections can be made on it readily, but its chief advantage is that it feeds its information into a computer at far greater speeds than do paper tapes or punched cards.

Magnetic ink characters placed on documents, such as checks, bank deposit slips, and other papers, can be read by machines in order to be processed. Bank checks bear such characters across the front at the bottom, usually in three groups. The first, at the left, identifies the bank's Federal Reserve District, the regional clearing house, and the bank itself on which the check is drawn, and the second group provides the number of the customer's account. Both groups are printed on the checks before they are delivered to the depositor. The third group, at the right, indicates the amount of the check, and is imprinted later by the bank or clearing house first receiving the check.

Processing. The term *processing* refers to the work performed by data processing equipment when it is activated by a program. It receives information as input material, classifies it, sorts it, makes arithmetical computations when needed, updates files of data, stores the revised information, and prepares output reports and documents if so directed.

Computer processing operations are discussed briefly in this chapter. Amazing progress has been made in recent years in the development of more versatile and more speedy machines.

Output. Information obtained from data processing equipment is known as *output*. Any acceptable means by which the coded information stored in such equipment can be converted into easily read characters is called an *output device*.

Output devices include electric typewriters that type rapidly one character at a time, line printers that print a line at a time at high speed, and other machines that use the information stored in data processing equipment to provide punched cards, punched paper tape, magnetic tape, and graphic presentation with cathode-ray (TV) tubes.

Output devices, as well as input devices, can be connected by wire with a distant computer. They are then known as *remote terminals*. There are remote computer installations where everything is present but the real calculating computer.

Output prepared for internal purposes generally consists of printed lists and reports (accounts receivable, depreciation schedule, sales by kinds of merchandise, financial statements, and so on) requested by management for its use, images on a TV screen, and punched cards and tape needed as input for further data processing purposes locally or for transmission to distant offices.

Output designed for external purposes consists principally of business documents, such as invoices, monthly statements to customers, and checks. Such documents, especially checks and the return portions of invoices, when issued in the form of punched cards, frequently bear the request, "Do not fold, spindle, staple, or mutilate," because they have been designed to serve as input devices when returned to the issuer.

DATA PROCESSING

Accounting data processing is only one kind of data processing. It is similar, basically, to other systems designed to process data for a multitude of statistical and other purposes, for census information, election results, tracking and giving instructions to space vehicles, air defense warning and other military uses, reporting stock market transactions, making airline and hotel reservations, conducting scientific experiments, and so on.

Processing of accounting data means doing the work necessary to produce the desired accounting records of business activities. An accounting system is a data processing system, whether it be operated manually or by machines.

Data processing by any nonmanual accounting system, such as a method which utilizes bookkeeping machines, punched card equipment, or electronic computers, is known generally as *automated data processing* (ADP), or *automatic data processing* (ADP), and sometimes as *integrated data processing* (IDP). Some authors restrict the definition of ADP or IDP to the processing of data by *automatic* equipment or *automated* equipment, either mechanical or electronic, that operates with a minimum of manual intervention. The designation IDP sometimes is limited to an ADP system designed to integrate the accounting information for an enterprise and provide a smooth flow of all of the accounting data needed for the operation of the business.

The term *electronic data processing* (EDP) is applied to a processing system operated by an electronic computer. Both terms ADP and EDP are applied indiscriminately at times to any automated data processing system.

BOOKKEEPING MACHINES

Machines are available with typewriter keyboards and adding and calculating mechanisms that can create several accounting records at one writing when recording a transaction. Examples are: (1) the writing of a payroll check with accompanying forms and carbon papers arranged so that the same information is written simultaneously on the check, on the employee's personal earnings record for the year, and on the payroll register or cash disbursements record, and (2) the posting of a sales invoice to a customer's account, while at the same time the information is being written on the customer's monthly statement to be sent at the end of the month, and on the sales journal.

Such machines, when compared with hand-written methods, add significantly to the speed with which a large volume of transactions can be recorded. They do not have the versatility of the large computers, but they are rendering satisfactory services to a great many enterprises.

Bookkeeping machines range in size from comparatively simple inexpensive combinations of typewriter and adding machine to extensive costly layouts that include punched cards, punched tape, and other features of electronic data processing machines, such as storage of information and recognition of magnetic ink characters.

PUNCHED CARD EQUIPMENT

Mechanization of data processing on a large scale was first attempted through the use of punched card equipment. Punched cards were developed in 1886 by Dr. Herman Hollerith, a statistician with the U.S. Census Bureau, in order to obtain more accurate and more varied census statistics than had been available previously.

Punched cards have revolutionized the processing of business data, making possible the recording of huge quantities of business transactions more efficiently than is possible by hand-written methods. At the same time, the cards produce more information of a helpful nature, at reasonable cost, than would be practicable by means of earlier accounting methods.

Punched card equipment includes the following more commonly employed machines: keypunch, reproducer, verifier, sorter, collator, calculator, and tabulator or high-speed printer.

Card Punching. Standard size cards to be punched contain eighty vertical columns, each divided into twelve punching positions. Holes are punched in designated positions on a card in accordance with a predetermined code designed for the particular system.

A *keypunch* punches the holes in the cards. It has a keyboard similar to that on a typewriter and is operated by depressing alphabetic, numeric, and special character keys. The information punched into the cards can then be read and processed by other machines. The simplest keypunch models punch holes only. Others have various automatic features, such as feeding and ejecting cards, duplicating entire cards or any part of them automatically, and printing characters along the top of a card simultaneously with the punching operation to facilitate manual reading of the card if desired.

Reproducing. A *reproducer* can transfer automatically to new cards all or any part of the information already punched into a set of cards. This ability is similar to that of some keypunch machines. A reproducer can also convert marks made on a card with a special pencil to holes in the same card.

Verifying. Because of the tendency of even the most capable operators to make an occasional error, the accuracy of the information punched into the cards must be verified. Punched cards that carry their information across the top in printed form can be verified by reading the material.

A *verifier* offers an efficient method of checking on the accuracy of the cards. An operator repeats the keypunching operations on a verifier, which notches each card as it passes through the machine to indicate whether it has been punched correctly or not. If an error has occurred, the keyboard of the machine becomes locked.

Sorting. Punched cards can be sorted and grouped in many ways to bring out the information they contain. A *sorter* provides the means for arranging the cards in a desired order, alphabetically, numerically, or according to some special characteristic, doing so at high speed and with a minimum of manual supervision. Sorters that read magnetized ink characters sort checks and other documents at a great saving of clerical labor.

Collating. A *collator* is a machine designed to merge two sets of punched cards into a single unified group. The two sets must have been sorted previously into the proper sequence so that the collator can insert each card from one set into the proper place in the other set.

Calculating. A *calculator* performs the necessary arithmetical operations on numerical data punched in the cards, such as prices per unit of merchandise or rates of depreciation on depreciable assets, in order to obtain desired totals. The calculator can then punch the results into the same cards.

Tabulating. A *tabulator,* or *printer,* converts into printed form all or any part of the information punched in cards or paper tape or carried on magnetic tape. It operates rapidly, printing a line at a time, and supplying subtotals and totals, if desired. Its output includes accounts receivable lists, merchandise inventory quantities and values, trial balances, financial statements, and a wide variety of other printed matter.

A tabulator operates according to instructions given to it either by the setting of dials or by the wiring of control panels. The panels can be wired to cause the machine to perform an almost endless number of different operations.

ELECTRONIC COMPUTERS

Since about the middle of the present century, there has been a tremendous growth in the employment of electronic computers for processing accounting data and a multitude of other kinds of data.

An electronic computer is a complicated electric calculator which operates at fantastic speeds, accepting input data, processing the data, and providing the results of the processing. It can add, subtract, multiply, and divide at speeds measured in microseconds, or millionths of a second; it receives coded information as input and sorts and stores it until needed; it combines new information with stored data in countless numbers of ways; it compares figures to determine whether one is larger, the same size, or smaller than another, and takes alternative actions depending on the results of the comparisons; and, it reports the results of its actions by means of printed reports or other forms of output discussed earlier in this chapter.

As previously stated, however, a computer can only follow instructions. Although it can make some decisions, such as choosing among alternative actions, yet it must be guided every step of the way and told exactly what to do as it operates, the steps having been planned in detail in advance and made a part of the program directing the machine.

Computer Processing Operations. An electronic computer has three basic components in addition to the input and output features already discussed. The components, all a part of the machine's processing operations, are: (1) a control unit, (2) a storage unit, and (3) an arithmetic unit.

Control. The *control* unit directs the operations of all the computer units, guided by a program which can be stored within the computer. Control tells the input device what information to accept and where to place it in the storage unit. It then directs the arithmetic unit to proceed, giving it step-by-step instructions from the stored program, telling it what operations to perform, where in storage to find the required information, and where to store the results. Finally, control directs the output device to report the results obtained, specifying the kind of information desired, where in storage to find it, and the method of reporting, whether by means of printed lists, punched cards, or other forms of output.

Thus, the control unit enables a computer to guide itself through intricate data processing operations, directed by a program containing detailed lists of instructions relating to the work to be done, and requiring a minimum amount of human intervention. Frequently, the only human effort required to run a computer is to mount tapes, see that the machine is supplied with whatever paper forms or cards may be needed for the output, and then push the start button on the computer's console.

Storage. The *storage* unit of a computer, also called the *memory* unit, accepts and retains information needed for later operations. It provides sections, or cells, numbered for ease of identification, in each of which can be stored a part of the data to be processed or instructions to be followed. When the program directs either that information be sent to storage or that it be retrieved, the instructions must indicate in detail the exact location within storage to which each item has been assigned.

Items held in storage can be used and reused as often as required. For example, a program for processing a payroll can direct that the same instructions be followed repeatedly, but each time with the name of a different employee, his hours, rate of pay, and deductions, until the entire payroll has been processed.

Another processing job can then be started, such as the recording of sales, or of purchases, which will require placing a new program in storage if it is not already there, providing the necessary paper forms or cards, and introducing the data to be processed.

Arithmetic. A computer's *arithmetic* unit performs the computations and makes the decisions that control requires, as directed by the program. It proceeds one step at a time, according to the detailed plan provided by the program, placing the intermediate results in storage until needed, and producing the final results with the characteristic speed of a computer, either storing the information for future reference or reporting it by means of the available output methods.

Time Sharing and EDP Service Centers. An electronic computer is costly, whether owned or rented by the user. The specially trained help needed to operate the equipment also is expensive. Smaller concerns, whose volume of business is too small to utilize the entire time of a computer, sometimes enter into time-sharing arrangements with other concerns, so that each can use the computer on a part-time basis and share the costs accordingly.

Computer services provided in numerous localities by banks, accounting firms, and EDP service centers on a fee basis offer small business units the operating efficiencies of electronic data processing.

Conclusion. Discussions of mechanized accounting in this chapter necessarily have been brief. The subject is an important one, however, especially for the accountant and for management, who are responsible for the type of service provided by the accounting department, and who, therefore, should welcome ideas for possible improvement of the service.

They should be aware, at least in a general way, of the contributions toward more efficient accounting records that are being made by data processing machines, the most spectacular of which are electronic computers, with their incredible speed, hitherto unobtainable accuracy, variety of information produced, and economy when the volume of business is large.

Accountants, especially those employed by large corporations or by accounting firms, generally will need more than a nodding acquaintance with the basic ideas underlying computer operations. They will need the ability to talk to a computer in a computer language such as COBOL.

With the introduction of high-speed data processing equipment, the accountant's role is changed. He spends less time on routine recording tasks and more on analysis and problem solving.

Data processing methods continue to improve, and the potential uses of automated equipment in accounting appear to be limitless. Increased effectiveness of such methods will increase also the opportunities for greater managerial control through accounting.

Appendix A: Illustrative Material

Material presented here will help the reader to apply and review some of the principles discussed elsewhere in the text. Numbers in parentheses indicate the pages on which related material appears.

CHART OF ACCOUNTS

An illustration of a numerical chart of accounts follows these comments. Such a chart is helpful to the bookkeeper and the accountant (41–46), and it may be indispensable if a machine accounting method is used which requires reference to the accounts by number (196). Many variations occur. A large company usually needs many more accounts than a small one, and a properly prepared list helps to identify them readily. Every chart of accounts should be planned so that it will meet the requirements of the specific company that adopts it.

In the illustrative chart, prepared for a manufacturing corporation, the principal groups of accounts begin with numbers as follows:

100	Assets
200	Liabilities
250	Proprietorship
275	Summary
300	Operating income
400	Manufacturing accounts
600	Selling expenses
700	General and administrative expenses

      800   Other income
      850   Other expenses
      900   Income taxes

Valuation accounts, representing deductions from the accounts to which they relate, are distinguished in this chart by having a zero as the first digit in each of their numbers.

If an account, such as salaries, appears in several expense groups, it is desirable, when convenient, to assign the same second and third digits to each such repeated account. This will help the bookkeeping department to identify them more readily. For example, in the following chart the salaries and wages accounts are numbered 401, 501, 601, and 701. When there are two or more salary accounts in one group, they are distinguished one from another by an additional digit following a decimal point, as indicated by account numbers 701.1, 701.2, and 701.3.

It is not necessary to list the numbers of group captions in a chart of accounts, although some accountants prefer to do so. The following chart shows the numbers of actual accounts only.

EUREKA MANUFACTURING COMPANY

CHART OF ACCOUNTS

Current Assets		(16)
100	Petty cash	(106, 107)
101	Cash in bank	
104	Temporary investments—marketable securities	(10, 11, 180)
111.1	Notes receivable, customers	
111.2	Notes receivable, others	
0111	Notes receivable discounted	
112.1	Accounts receivable, customers	
112.2	Accounts receivable, others	
116	Loans to employees	
0119	Allowance for doubtful notes and accounts	(83)
124	Accrued interest receivable	(75)
125	Accrued rent receivable	
130.1	Inventories of raw materials	(162)
130.2	Inventories of goods in process	
130.3	Inventories of finished goods	
135	Prepaid interest expense	(16, 75)
136	Unexpired insurance	(11, 39, 76)
137	Prepaid taxes and licenses	
145	Office supplies on hand	(76)

Fixed Assets (15–17)
150.1 Investments in affiliated companies (180)
150.2 Other long-term investments
155 Land
160 Building, factory
0160 Allowance for depreciation of factory building (78, 79)
161 Building, office
0161 Allowance for depreciation of office building
165 Machinery and equipment
0165 Allowance for depreciation of machinery and equipment
170 Office furniture and fixtures
0170 Allowance for depreciation of office furniture and fixtures
175 Patterns and drawings
0175 Allowance for depreciation of patterns and drawings

Other Assets
180 Sinking fund in hands of trustee (146, 148)
181 Goodwill (166)
182 Patents
0182 Allowance for amortization of patents
184 Trademarks
0184 Allowance for amortization of trademarks
186 Organization expense (123, 166)
0186 Allowance for amortization of organization expense
188 Unamortized discount on bonds payable

Current Liabilities
200.1 Notes payable, banks
200.2 Notes payable, others
201 Accounts payable, trade creditors
205 Accrued wages payable
206 Accrued interest payable (75)
207 Accrued payroll taxes
208 Accrued income taxes
209 Other accrued expenses
215 Deferred rent income
216 Other deferred income
220 Advances from stockholders, officers, and employees
225 Dividends payable (135)
226 Other current liabilities

Fixed Liabilities
230 Mortgages payable
235 Bonds payable (140–145)
240 Unamortized premium on bonds payable (140–143)
245 Other long-term liabilities

Owners' Equity

250	Capital stock, preferred	(124, 125)
0250	Treasury stock, preferred	(130)
251	Capital stock, common	
255	Paid-in capital above par value of stock	(128, 129)
256	Donated capital	(130–132)
258	Appropriation (or reserve) for plant extension	(146, 148)
259	Appropriation (or reserve) for contingencies	(147–148)
260	Retained earnings unappropriated	(133)

Summary

275	Manufacturing summary	
276	Income summary account	(38, 62, 133)

Operating Income (20)

300	Sales, home office	
0300.1	Sales returns and allowances, home office	
0300.2	Sales discounts, home office	
305	Sales, branch office	(174)

Manufacturing Costs (162–166)

400	Purchases of raw materials	
0400.1	Purchase returns and allowances	
0400.2	Purchase discounts	
400.5	Transportation in, or freight and cartage in	
401	Salaries and wages, purchasing department	
410	Utilities, purchasing department	
416	Repairs and maintenance, purchasing department equipment	
430	Depreciation of purchasing department equipment	
450	Taxes, purchasing department	
460	Supplies used, purchasing department	
480	Miscellaneous purchasing department expenses	
490	Receiving department expenses	
501.1	Direct labor, production department 1	
501.2	Direct labor, production department 2	
501.3	Indirect labor	(164, 165)
510	Utilities, factory	
516.1	Repairs and maintenance of factory building	
516.2	Repairs and maintenance of machinery	
530.1	Depreciation of factory building	
530.2	Depreciation of factory equipment	
530.3	Amortization of patents	
535	Royalties	
550	Property taxes, factory	
560	Factory supplies used	
580	Sundry factory expenses	

Selling Expenses   (28)
601.1	Salaries and commissions, salesmen
601.2	Salaries and commissions, sales supervision
601.3	Clerical salaries, sales department
605	Traveling expenses, salesmen
607	Advertising and samples
610	Utilities, sales department
616	Repairs and maintenance of sales equipment
630.1	Depreciation of sales office building
630.2	Depreciation of sales department equipment
650	Property taxes, sales department
660	Sales department supplies used
665	Freight and cartage outward
680	Sundry selling expenses

General and Administrative Expenses   (28, 29)
701.1	Officers' salaries
701.2	Directors' fees
701.3	Office salaries
703	Legal and accounting fees
705	Traveling expenses, general
710	Utilities, general office
716	Repairs and maintenance of general office equipment
730.1	Depreciation of building, general office
730.2	Depreciation of general office equipment
750	Taxes and licenses, general office
753	Postage and express, general office
755	Printing and stationery, general office
760	General office supplies used
770	Bad debts expense
780	Sundry administrative expenses

Other Income   (24, 26, 29)
808	Interest earned
809	Dividends received
810	Rent income
811	Sales of scrap
840	Miscellaneous nonoperating income (185)

Other Expenses
850	Taxes on investment property
855	Interest expense (29, 75)
880	Miscellaneous nonoperating expenses
900	Income taxes

WORK SHEET AND FINANCIAL STATEMENTS

At the close of an accounting period, or whenever financial statements are required, the bookkeeper generally will take a trial balance of the unadjusted accounts in the ledger, listing the amounts in debit and credit columns on a work sheet. Adjustments for inventories, accruals, and other necessary changes in the accounts are shown in the next two columns. Additional columns provide space for an adjusted trial balance, if desired, and for the segregation of balance sheet and income statement items (59–61).

Four columns will suffice for the financial statement items, but additional columns can provide helpful subclassifications at times. For example, if two columns were added to the work sheet which follows, they could show separately the cost of goods manufactured and sold to simplify preparation of a schedule with that title as part of the financial report.

An eight-column work sheet for the Eureka Manufacturing Company follows. Note that the accounts are listed in the preceding chart of accounts for this company. The chart contains a number of accounts that do not appear on the work sheet. If the company is expanding, it will be planning for the needs of the near future which conceivably will include use of all of these accounts.

Following the work sheet, the next page contains a comparative balance sheet and additional information needed for preparation of the funds statement.

Then the next five pages contain the Eureka Manufacturing Company's balance sheet, income statement, and statement of changes in financial position, which are based on the work sheet illustrated.

Exhibit A, the balance sheet, gives in some detail the assets, liabilities, and proprietorship at the close of the accounting period only. Balance sheets in the published financial reports of large corporations usually appear in highly condensed comparative form, showing totals at the ends of both the current year and

Eureka Manufacturing Company
Work Sheet
For Year Ended May 31, 19.. — Page 1

#	Account Title	Trial Balance Dr.	Trial Balance Cr.	Adjustments Dr.	Adjustments Cr.	Income Statement Dr.	Income Statement Cr.	Balance Sheet Dr.	Balance Sheet Cr.
1	Petty cash	500						500	
2	Cash in banks	17600						17600	
3	Marketable securities	5000						5000	
4	Notes receivable, customers	4000						4000	
5	Accounts receivable, customers	31000						31000	
6	Allowance for doubtful receivables		100	(3) 900					1000
7	Accrued interest receivable, customers	—		(4) 60				60	
8	Inventories of raw materials	19000		(2) 12000(1)	19000			12000	
9	Inventories of goods in process	27250		(2) 21000	27250			21000	
10	Inventories of finished goods	25000		(2) 24000	25000			24000	
11	Prepaid taxes and insurance	4270			(5) 1440			2830	
12	Office supplies on hand	1520			(6) 600			920	
13	Investment in stock of affiliated companies	10000						10000	
14	Land	21300						21300	
15	Building	95000						95000	
16	Allowance for depreciation of building		21925		(7) 2375				24300
17	Factory machinery and equipment	91000						96000	
18	Allowance for depreciation of machinery and equipment		22400		(8) 8600				31000
19	Office equipment	9000						9000	
20	Allowance for depreciation of office equipment		3000		(9) 900				3900
21	Patents	13900						13900	
22	Allowance for amortization of patents		6195		(10) 815				7000
23	Accounts payable, trade creditors		8200						8200
24	Accrued wages payable		3000						3000
25	Accrued taxes payable		500						500
26	Income taxes payable				(11) 7110				7110
27	Mortgage payable		20000						20000
28	Capital stock, common		200000						200000
29	Additional paid-in capital		20000						20000
30	Retained earnings		26000						26000
31	Dividends declared	21000						21000	
32	Income summary, raw materials inventory			(1) 16000	(2) 12000	16000	12000		
33	Income summary, goods in process inventory			(1) 27250	(2) 21000	27250	21000		
34	Income summary, finished goods inventory			(1) 35000	(2) 24000	25000	24000		
35	Sales		415500				415500		
36	Sales returns and allowances	2500				2500			
37	Sales discounts	3000				3000			
38	Purchases of raw materials	116300				116300			
39	Purchase returns and allowances		800				800		
40	Totals carried forward	511060	747510	125910	140010	190050	473300	376612	357910

Eureka Manufacturing Company
Work Sheet
For Year Ended May 31, 19.. — Page 2

Account Titles	Trial Balance Dr.	Trial Balance Cr.	Adjustments Dr.	Adjustments Cr.	Income Statement Dr.	Income Statement Cr.	Balance Sheet Dr.	Balance Sheet Cr.
Totals brought forward	511,060	747,510	1,253.0	149,010	190,050	473,300	376,010	351,910
Purchase discounts		600				1,600		
Transportation in	4,150				1,150			
Direct labor, production department	97,240				97,240			
Indirect labor	22,350				22,350			
Factory utilities	5,000				5,000			
Machinery repairs and maintenance	8,700				8,700			
Depreciation of building, factory	—		(7) 1,725		1,725			
Depreciation of machinery and equipment	—		(8) 8,400		8,400			
Amortization of patents	—		(10) 915		915			
Royalties	3,990				5,490			
Property taxes	4,570		(9) 1,300		3,740			
Factory supplies used	4,600		(6) 500		5,100			
Miscellaneous factory expense	900				900			
Labor and commissions, salesmen	23,400				23,400			
Traveling expenses, salesmen	7,000				7,000			
Advertising	10,000				10,000			
Utilities, sales department	560				560			
Depreciation of building, sales office	—		(7) 100		100			
Depreciation of sales equipment	—		(9) 200		200			
Property taxes	65		(5) 30		95			
Sales department supplies used	450		(6) 50		505			
Freight and cartage outward	1,210				1,210			
Miscellaneous selling expense	770				990			
Salaries, officers	3,000				3,000			
Salaries, office	12,000				12,000			
Utilities, general office	670				670			
Depreciation of building, general office	—		(7) 350		350			
Depreciation of equipment, general office	—		(9) 700		700			
Taxes and licenses, general	320		(5) 120		560			
Office supplies, general office	350		(6) 50		400			
Bad debts expense	—		(3) 900		990			
Miscellaneous administrative expense	240				240			
Interest income				(4) 60		700		
Dividends received		640				1,000		
Interest expense	1,400				1,400			
Income taxes		1,000			7,110			
	750,750	750,750	149,070	149,070	453,500	476,600	376,010	351,910
Net income					24,100			24,100
					476,600	476,600	376,010	376,010

the preceding year, and often with amounts rounded off to the nearest thousand dollars.

Exhibit B, the income statement, is prevented from spreading over two pages by placing the items relating to cost of goods manufactured and sold on a separate schedule, Exhibit C, and using its total as one item on the income statement accompanied by a reference indicating that it came from Exhibit C.

Exhibit D, the statement of changes in financial position, is the third financial statement that is required, generally, to accompany the balance sheet and income statement.

Supplementary information given below is needed for preparation of the statement of changes in financial position.

EUREKA MANUFACTURING COMPANY

COMPARATIVE BALANCE SHEET
MAY 31, CURRENT YEAR, AND MAY 31, PRECEDING YEAR

	May 31		Differences	
ASSETS	Current Year	Preceding Year	Debit	Credit
Cash	$ 18,100	$ 19,100		$ 1,000
Marketable securities	5,000	5,000		
Receivables (Net)	34,060	26,960	$ 7,100	
Inventories	57,000	68,250		11,250
Prepaid expenses	3,750	3,000	750	
Stock in affiliated companies	10,000	2,000	8,000	
Land	21,300	24,300	7,000	10,000
Building	95,000	95,000		
Factory machinery and equipment	86,000	86,000		
Office equipment	9,000	9,000		
Patents (Net)	6,800	7,615		815
Accumulated depreciation, plant and equipment	(59,100)	(47,225)		11,875
	$286,910	$299,000		
LIABILITIES AND CAPITAL				
Current payables	$ 18,810	$ 19,000	190	
Mortgage payable	20,000	24,000	4,000	
Bonds payable	—	10,000	10,000	
Capital stock, common	200,000	200,000		
Paid-in capital	20,000	20,000		
Retained earnings	28,100	26,000		2,100
	$286,910	$299,000	$37,040	$37,040

Additional data:
1. Capital stock of affiliated companies was purchased during the year for $8,000 cash
2. Land was purchased during the year for $7,000 cash
3. A parcel of land which cost $10,000 was exchanged for the

EUREKA MANUFAC

BALANCE
MAY

ASSETS

Current Assets
Cash on hand and in banks | | $18,100
Marketable securities, at cost (market value, $5,500) | | 5,000
Receivables
Notes receivable, customers | $ 4,000 |
Accounts receivable, customers | 31,000 |
Total | $35,000 |
Less allowance for doubtful receivables | 1,000 | 34,000
Accrued interest receivable | | 60
Inventories
Raw materials | $12,000 |
Goods in process | 21,000 |
Finished goods | 24,000 | 57,000
Prepaid expenses
Prepaid taxes and licenses | $ 2,830 |
Office supplies on hand | 920 | 3,750
Total current assets | | $117,910

Investments
Stock of affiliated companies | | 10,000

Plant and Equipment
Land | | $21,300
Building | $95,000 |
Less accumulated depreciation | 24,200 | 70,800
Factory machinery and equipment | $86,000 |
Less accumulated depreciation | 31,000 | 55,000
Office equipment | $9,000 |
Less accumulated depreciation | 3,900 | 5,100
Total plant and equipment | | 152,200

Intangible Assets
Patents | $13,800 |
Less accumulated amortization | 7,000 | 6,800
Total Assets | | $286,910

remaining outstanding bonds payable having a face value
of $10,000

4. A cash payment of $4,000 reduced the mortgage payable
balance to $20,000

5. Dividends of $22,000 were declared and paid.

TURING COMPANY

EXHIBIT A

SHEET
31, 19--

LIABILITIES AND STOCKHOLDERS' EQUITY

Current Liabilities			
Accounts payable, trade creditors		$ 8,200	
Accrued wages payable		3,000	
Payroll taxes payable		500	
Income taxes payable		7,110	
Total current liabilities			$ 18,810
Long-term Liabilities			
Mortgage payable, due 1990			20,000
Total liabilities			$38,810
Stockholders' Equity			
Capital stock, common, 2,000 shares autho-rized, issued, and outstanding, $100 par value		$200,000	
Additional paid-in capital		20,000	
Retained earnings			
Balance, June 1, 19--	$26,000		
Net income for the year (Exhibit B)	24,100		
Total	$50,100		
Less dividends declared	22,000		
Retained earnings, May 31, 19--		28,100	
Total stockholders' equity			248,100
Total Liabilities and Stockholders' Equity			$286,910

EUREKA MANUFACTURING COMPANY

EXHIBIT B

INCOME STATEMENT
FOR THE YEAR ENDED MAY 31, 19--

Sales			$415,500
Sales returns and allowances		$ 2,500	
Sales discounts		3,000	5,500
Net sales			$410,000
Cost of goods manufactured and sold (Exhibit C)			281,530
Gross profit on sales			$128,470
Operating expenses			
Selling expenses			
Salaries and commissions, salesmen	$27,480		
Traveling expenses, salesmen	9,000		
Advertising	10,000		
Utilities	560		
Depreciation, sales office portion of building	100		
Depreciation, sales office equipment	200		
Property taxes	95		
Sales department supplies used	505		
Freight and cartage outward	1,210		
Miscellaneous selling expenses	990	50,140	
General and administrative expenses			
Salaries, officers	$31,000		
Salaries, office	12,000		
Utilities	670		
Depreciation, general office portion of building	350		
Depreciation, general office equipment	700		
Taxes and licenses	560		
General office supplies used	400		
Bad debts expense	900		
Miscellaneous administrative expenses	840	47,420	97,560
Net income from operations			$ 30,910
Interest income	$ 700		
Dividends received	1,000	$ 1,700	
Interest expense		1,400	300
Net income before income taxes			$ 31,210
Income taxes			7,110
Net income			$ 24,100

EUREKA MANUFACTURING COMPANY
EXHIBIT C

STATEMENT OF COST OF GOODS MANUFACTURED AND SOLD
FOR THE YEAR ENDED MAY 31, 19--

Raw materials			
Beginning raw materials inventory			$ 16,000
Purchases of raw materials		$116,300	
Purchase returns and allowances	$ 800		
Purchase discounts	1,600	2,400	
Net purchases		$113,900	
Transportation in		1,150	115,050
Raw materials available for use			$131,050
Ending raw materials inventory			12,000
Cost of raw materials used			$119,050
Direct labor, production department			92,240
Factory overhead			
Indirect labor		$ 22,350	
Factory utilities		5,080	
Machinery repairs and maintenance		8,720	
Depreciation expenses			
Factory portion of building		1,925	
Machinery and equipment		8,600	
Amortization of patents		815	
Royalties		5,840	
Property taxes		3,760	
Factory supplies used		5,100	
Miscellaneous factory expenses		800	
Total factory overhead			62,990
Total manufacturing costs			$274,280
Beginning goods in process inventory			27,250
Total goods in process during the year			$301,530
Ending goods in process inventory			21,000
Cost of goods manufactured			$280,530
Beginning finished goods inventory			25,000
Total cost of finished goods available for sale			$305,530
Ending finished goods inventory			24,000
Total cost of goods manufactured and sold			$281,530

EUREKA MANUFACTURING COMPANY

EXHIBIT D

STATEMENT OF CHANGES IN FINANCIAL POSITION
FOR THE YEAR ENDED MAY 31, 19--

Sources of funds		
Operations		
Net income	$24,100	
Add expenses not requiring funds		
Depreciation of building and equipment	11,875	
Amortization of patents	815	$36,790
Transfer of land costing $10,000 to pay balance due on bonds payable		10,000
Total funds provided		$46,790
Application of funds		
Purchase of stock of affiliated companies	$ 8,000	
Purchase of land	7,000	
Retirement of bonds payable by transfer of land	10,000	
Payment on mortgage payable	4,000	
Payment of cash dividends	22,000	
Total funds applied		51,000
Decrease in working capital		$4,210

EUREKA MANUFACTURING COMPANY

SCHEDULE OF CHANGES IN WORKING CAPITAL
FOR THE YEAR ENDED MAY 31, 19--

	End of Year	Beginning of Year	Working Capital Increase	Decrease
Cash	$18,100	$19,100		$ 1,000
Marketable securities	5,000	5,000		
Receivables (Net)	34,060	26,960	$ 7,100	
Inventories	57,000	68,250		11,250
Prepaid expenses	3,750	3,000	750	
Current payables	18,810	19,000	190	
			$ 8,040	$12,250
Decrease in working capital			4,210	
			$12,250	$12,250

Appendix B: Sample Examination Questions and Answers

Sample questions taken from accounting examinations may be useful to the reader in reviewing his accounting knowledge. There are two principal kinds of questions in an accounting examination. They are the essay or discussion type and the objective or short-answer type.

The first group of questions (Part 1) consists of the essay or discussion type. No answers are given, but each question is followed by figures in parentheses referring to the page or pages in this book on which an answer to the question can be found. The remaining groups (Part 2) consist of the objective or short-answer type of questions. Answers and references to pages in this book are indicated for these questions on page 230.

PART 1

Instructions. Answer the questions in the following group fully, but do not use more words than necessary. Be sure that each answer indicates your understanding of the material covered.

1. (a) Define the terms *bookkeeping* and *accounting,* and indicate how they differ. (1, 2)

   (b) What is the primary purpose of accounting? (2)

2. List the classes of assets and liabilities, and describe each class briefly. (16, 17)

3. (a) Describe an income statement. (22–25)

   (b) Give a brief description of each of the items that make up the cost of goods sold section of an income statement. (27, 28)

4. (a) How is the balance sheet affected by a business transaction? (31, 32)
(b) Prepare a T account for each of five classes of accounts, and, with the help of plus and minus signs, show which side of each account is used for increases and which side for decreases. (34)
5. (a) What is meant by the financial statement sequence of accounts in the ledger? (42)
(b) Explain one method of preparing a trial balance of ledger accounts. (47)
6. (a) Describe the processes of journalizing and of posting. (52–55)
(b) Explain the relationship between the journal and the ledger. (55)
7. (a) How does the accrual basis of accounting differ from the cash basis? (56)
(b) List the steps in the accounting cycle. (64)
8. (a) Explain the gross profit method for estimating the value of an inventory. (70)
(b) A popular method for the valuation of inventories is cost or market, whichever is lower. Discuss. (73, 74)
9. (a) Explain the use of a valuation account. (77, 78)
(b) Define *depreciation*, and explain one method of computing it. (78–81)
10. (a) List the advantages of special journals. (90, 91)
(b) How can a subsidiary ledger be converted into a self-balancing ledger? (94)
11. (a) Discuss the important of business papers. (102, 103)
(b) Why should a bank reconcilation be prepared? (106)
12. Is the voucher register a journal or a ledger? Explain briefly. (110, 111)
13. (a) Describe the proprietary accounts for a single proprietorship and for a partnership. (114, 118)
(b) Discuss the distribution of partnership profits and losses. (119)
14. (a) What journal entries are made to record sales by a corporation of its own previously unissued capital stock? (126–128)

(b) What disposition is made of a corporation's profit or loss at the close of an accounting period?   (133–135)

15. (a) How do nominal and effective interest rates affect the price of bonds?   (139, 140)

(b) What is an appropriation of retained earnings? (148)

16. What is the significance of the statement of changes in financial position?   (151)

17. How do the financial statements reveal whether an enterprise is a manufacturing or a mercantile concern?

(162–169)

18. Discuss the preparation of financial statements for an enterprise with branches.   (175, 176)

19. Name five kinds of discount, and discuss one of them briefly.   (181–184)

20. How are percentages and ratios used in the analysis of financial statements?   (189–191)

21. (a) What is a program for an electronic computer? (197)

(b) What is the significance of the letters EDP?   (201)

PART 2

I. Instructions. In each of the following statements, select from the answers given the one that *best* answers or completes the statement. More than one answer may apply, but one answer will be the best. Indicate your choice by underscoring the number of the answer.

1. Cash appears on the financial statements as:
   1. An asset
   2. A proprietary account
   3. A current asset
   4. A reserve account
   5. A capital account

2. By gross profit we mean:
   1. Sales minus cost of goods sold
   2. Sales minus net profit on sales
   3. Gross margin minus cost of goods sold
   4. Gross trading profit minus operating expenses
   5. Sales minus selling expenses

3. Which of the following would require a debit entry?
   1. Increase in an income account
   2. Increase in a proprietorship account
   3. Increase in a liability account
   4. Increase in an asset account
4. A statement showing the items which make up the difference between the bank statement and the cash account is known as:
   1. An adjustment sheet
   2. A reconciliation of bank balance
   3. An income statement
   4. A funds statement
5. Company X capital stock having a par value of $1,000 is donated to Company X. The proper entry is:
   1. Debit capital stock, credit donated capital
   2. Debit donated capital, credit treasury stock
   3. Debit treasury stock, credit donated capital
   4. Debit capital stock, credit retained earnings
   5. Debit treasury stock, credit paid-in capital
6. Stock referred to above was reissued for $1,200 cash. The proper entry is:
   1. Debit cash and donated capital, credit treasury stock
   2. Debit cash, credit treasury stock and donated capital
   3. Debit cash, credit treasury stock
   4. Debit cash, credit treasury stock and retained earnings
   5. Debit cash and retained earnings, credit treasury stock
7. A promise under seal to pay a definite sum of money at a stated time and to pay interest at a stipulated rate is known as:
   1. A preferred stock
   2. A promissory note
   3. A mortgage payable
   4. A bond
   5. A common stock

8. Periodic amortization of premium on bonds payable requires adjustment of:
   1. Retained earnings
   2. Paid-in capital
   3. Allowance for sinking fund
   4. Interest income
   5. Interest expense
9. The purpose of an appropriation for bond sinking fund is:
   1. To set aside cash for payment of the bonds at maturity
   2. To provide for payment of interest on the bonds
   3. To serve as a valuation reserve
   4. To retain earnings and provide more security for the bonds
   5. To increase the proprietorship total on the balance sheet
10. The *current ratio* is the ratio of:
    1. Net sales to net profit
    2. Net sales to proprietorship
    3. Current assets to current liabilities
    4. Current assets to total assets
    5. Current liabilities to current assets

II. Instructions. Statements in this section are either true or false. If a statement is true, place a plus sign to the left of the number of the statement. If it is false, place a zero to the left of the number of the statement.

1. Accounting involves the recording of business transactions in monetary terms.
2. Posting is done by making entries in the journal.
3. It is desirable to record loss from bad debts before ascertaining definitely which specific accounts will be uncollectible.
4. Use of special journals retards the division of labor, making it difficult to distribute the work among the bookkeepers.
5. When a voucher register is used, a purchase journal and an accounts payable ledger are no longer necessary.

6. C, who purchased a 25 per cent interest in a partnership composed of A and B, is entitled to 25 per cent of the firm's profits in the absence of any agreement relating to the distribution of profits.

7. Market value of stock can be computed from the information shown on the balance sheet.

8. A debit balance in an overhead account indicates that overhead was underabsorbed.

9. The debit balance in one reciprocal account must equal the credit balance in the other, at the close of an accounting period.

10. The expression 2/10, n/30, means that a discount of 2 per cent is to be granted if payment is made within 30 days.

III. Instructions. Indicate by a plus sign each answer that is correct, and by a zero each answer that is wrong. Place the marks to the left of the questions.

1. A purpose of the closing entries is:
   a. To facilitate posting and taking the trial balance
   b. To close the nominal accounts so that they may be used to accumulate only the costs or revenue of the future
   c. To balance the suspense accounts so that they may be used to accumulate only the costs or revenue of the future
   d. To transfer the net result of the period from the expense and income accounts to a proprietorship account

2. Profit for the year would be overstated if adjusting entries were omitted for:
   a. Accrued wages payable
   b. Interest accrued on notes receivable
   c. Depreciation
   d. Accrued taxes payable
   e. Bad debts

IV. Instructions. Several books of original entry are listed below, each of which is designated by one or two letters. Following them is a series of transactions. At the left of the number of each transaction, write the letter or letters indicating the journal in which the transaction should ordinarily be recorded. This is not a complete list of transactions of the business.

Books of original entry:

CD   Cash disbursements journal
CR   Cash receipts journal
J   General journal
P   Purchase journal
S   Sales journal

Transactions:

1. J. J. Jones invested cash in the television business.
2. Purchased television sets, radios, and records from R. T. Smith on account. Terms, 2/10, n/30.
3. Purchased an adding machine for cash.
4. Paid rent for the month.
5. Sold phonograph records to L. Perry on account.
6. Returned some poor quality merchandise to R. T. Smith for credit.
7. Issued a note to R. T. Smith in payment of his account.
8. Withdrew a small amount of cash for personal use.
9. Adjusted the merchandise inventory account.
10. Closed the income summary account.

Answers to Part 2

I

Ques.	Ans.	Text Ref.	Ques.	Ans.	Text Ref.
1	3	16	6	2	131
2	1	28	7	4	137
3	4	34	8	5	141
4	2	106	9	4	148
5	3	131	10	3	190

II

Stmt.	Ans.	Text Ref.	Stmt.	Ans.	Text Ref.
1	+	1	6	0	119
2	0	54	7	0	126
3	+	82	8	+	165
4	0	95	9	+	175
5	+	110, 111	10	0	181

III

Stmt.	Ans.	Text Ref.	Stmt.	Ans.	Text Ref.
1a	0	62	2a	+	75–82
1b	+	62	2b	0	75–82
1c	0	39	2c	+	75–82
1d	+	62	2d	+	75–82
			2e	+	75–82

IV

Text Reference: pp. 88–100

Trans.	Ans.	Trans.	Ans.	Trans.	Ans.
1	CR	4	CD	8	CD
2	P	5	S	9	J
3	CD	6	J	10	J
		7	J		

Index

Abstract of accounts, 95, 99, 191
Abstract of vouchers payable, 111
Acceptance, trade, 105
Account form and construction, 36, 37
Accountant, 5, 25, 162, 194, 206, 207, 209, 210
Accountant, certified public, 5, 194
Accountant, cost, 162, 194
Accountants Digest, 195
Accounting: accrual method, 56, 57, 75, 156–159; and book-keeping, 2, 4, 5; and business management, 2, 5, 8, 188–195; and modern business, 6; auditing, 5; branch, 174–176; budgetary, 5, 193; cash method, 56, 156, 157; controllership, 5; cost, 5, 161–171; cycle, 64; data processing, 201; defined, 1; departmental, 42, 172, 173; development, 1, 6–8; distinguished from bookkeeping, 2; entity, 4; equation, 10, 13, 14, 34, 35; fields, 5; fundamental rule, 35, 52; funds, 149, 150; general, 5; governmental and institutional, 6; how to study, ix; industrial, 161–171; in modern business, 4–8; literature, 194, 195; machine applications, 196; management services, 6; mechanized, 187, 196–207; nature of, 1; organizations, 194; period, 22, 57; purpose, 2; relationship to other fields, 8; reserves, 149; sales, 187; subsidiaries, 177–179; sys-

tem building and revision, 5, 45; tax, 6, 7; tool of management, 9; universal need for, 4; work classified, 5, 6, 194
Accounting Review, 195
Accounts, 31–40; abstract of, 95, 99, 191; aging, 83; alphabetical order, 42; ancillary, 39; arrangement, 41–45, 92; asset reduction, 77; balance, 38, 47, 62; balance sheet, 33, 38, 39; balancing, 94, 166; balancing process, 37, 38, 62, 63; branch, 174–176; capital, *see* Proprietorship, accounts; capital stock, 121–136; capital stock subscribed, 127, 128; card of, 45, 46; changes in proprietorship, 18, 38–40; chart of, 44, 46, 209–213; classes, 39–40; classification, 41–47; codification, 43–46, 209–213; columnar ledger, 87, 94; contra, *see* Contra account; controlling, *see* Controlling account; credit balance, 38; creditors, 92, 94; current, 12, 13, 114, 118, 123; customers, 42, 92, 94; debit balance, 38; defined, 33, 36; departmental, 42, 172, 173; described, 33, 34; drawing, 12, 13, 114, 118, 123; economic, 39; elements, 33, 35, 38, 39, 58; expense, *see* Expense; explanatory, 39; factory ledger, 166, 167; fictitious, 39; financial statement sequence, or order, 42, 46; footing, 37, 38; form

Advanced discussion of accounts, 180–187
Advances, intercompany, 178
Affiliated companies, 178
Agency, 174
Agency, mutual, 115, 116
Aging accounts receivable, 83
All-inclusive income statement, 23
Allowance: accounting for, 149; a contra account, 77, 78, 81, 82, 147; accrued liability, 147, 149; adjustments, 78; bad debts, 77, 78, 83, 147; balance sheet presentation, 132, 133, 148–150; collection losses, 83; credit losses, 83; depletion, 78, 82, 147; depreciation, 15, 78, 79, 81, 102, 147, 153, 217, 218; doubtful receivables, 83; exhaustion, 78; reserve, 78, 81, 147; uncollectible notes and accounts, 83; uncollectible taxes, 146
Alphabetical order of accounts, 42
American Accounting Association, 194
American Institute of Certified Public Accountants, 23, 194
American Society of Women Accountants, 194
American Woman's Society of Certified Public Accountants, 194
Amortization: bond premium and discount, 140–145; bond table method; 142, 143; bonds outstanding method, 142; defined, 141; interest method, 142; mathematical formulas, 142, 143; recording, 141–145; schedule, 143; straight-line, 142
Analysis of financial statements, 189–193
Analysis of sales, 192
Analysis of working capital changes, 152
Analytical record. See Ledger
Ancient records, 1
Ancillary accounts, 39

Answers to examination questions, 230
Application of funds statement, 152
Appraisal capital, 132, 133
Appropriated capital, 149
Appropriated retained earnings, 133, 134, 146–150
Appropriated surplus, 132, 146
Appropriations: accrued liability, 147, 149; contingencies, 148; extension, 146, 148; retained earnings, 133, 134, 146–150; retirement of long-term debt, 148; retirement of preferred stock, 148; sinking fund, 148; surplus reserves, 133, 134
Approval sales, 185, 186
Arrangement of accounts, 41–45, 92
Articles of copartnership, 116, 119
Asset expenditure, 184
Asset reduction account, 77, 147
Asset valuation account, 147
Assets: accounts receivable, 11; accrued receivables, 11; active, 16; assets, liabilities, and capital statement, 13; bills receivable, 11; book value, 149, 194; buildings, 11, 17; capital, 16, 17, 184, 185; changes, 18, 31, 32, 34, 35; circulating 16; classification, 16, 17; conversion, 18, 31; copyrights, 11, 166; current, 16; deferred, see Expense, deferred; defined, 10, 11; delivery equipment, 11; depreciation, 18, 78–82; equipment, 11, 17; exchange, 31; exhaustive, 82; fabrication, 18; fixed, 14–17, 102, 153, 168, 169, 184, 211, 217, 218; floating, 16; formulas, 166; franchises, 11, 166; fully pledged, 194; furniture and fixtures, 11; goodwill, 11, 118, 166, 178; intangible, 10, 11, 17, 166, 168; land, 11, 15, 153, 217, 218; leaseholds, 11, 166; liquid, 16; long-term investments, 11, 143; machinery, 11, 17, 42, 102; marketable securi-

Gross income, 19, 20, 26, 28
Gross margin on sales, 19, 28
Gross profit: a computed total, 19, 26, 28, 29; deferred, 19, 28; estimated inventory method, 70; other titles, 19, 28
Gross receipts from operations, 19
Gross revenue, 19
Gross sales, 19, 27

Hidden reserve, 148
Historical cost, 3, 147
Holding company, 176–179
Home office account, 94, 175
How to study accounting, ix

Impersonal account, 39
Imprest fund, 107, 146
Imprest system, 107
Inadequacy, 78
Income: account, an income statement, 22; accounts, temporary proprietorship, 12, 13, 34, 39, 40, 62; accrued, 57–59, 63, 64, 75–77; and capital account statement, 22; and expense statement, 22; changes, 22, 32; classification, 24–30, 162–166; commissions, 76; deferred, 12, 17, 57–59, 63, 64, 75–77, 183; defined, 19; departmental, 172–174; effect on proprietorship, 34; extraneous, 29; extraordinary, 20, 22, 23, 133; financial and other, 29; financial management, 29; gross, 19, 20, 26, 28; intercompany, 179; interest, 29, 75, 183; net, 19–26, 29, 30, 133; net operating, 20, 23–26, 29; nonoperating, 20, 24, 29, 30, 168, 185; operating, 20, 29, 34; operating gross, 20; other, 24, 26, 29; outside, 29; prepaid, see Income, deferred; purchase discount, see Purchase discount; received in advance, see Income, deferred; rent, 29, 76; revenue, 19, 22, 184; royalties, 76; sales, 19; sheet, an income statement, 22; summary account, 38, 62, 133, 166; temporary proprietorship, 12, 13, 34,

39, 40, 62; unearned, see Income deferred
Income statement, 2, 3, 19–30; account form, 24; all-inclusive, 23; capital gains and losses, 185; classification of items, 24–30, 162–166; combined, 177; comparative, 168, 191; condensed, 154, 168; consolidated, 177–179; conversion to cash basis, 157; cost of goods manufactured and sold, 27, 165–168, 213, 216, 219, 220; cumulative, 191; current operating, 22, 23; defined, 3, 22; departmental, 173; discounts, 26–29, 181; estimated, 193; examples, 25, 26, 154, 220, 221; financial statement, 2, 3, 13, 19; form, 23–26, 154, 220, 221; horizontal form, 24; importance, 13, 22, 151; major financial statement, 2, 3, 19, 151; manufacturing enterprise, 25, 27, 167, 168, 220, 221; mercantile business, 24–30, 154, 167; multiple-step, 24–30, 220, 221; narrative form, 24; nonoperating items, 185; other income and other expenses, 24, 26, 29; other titles, 22; percentages, 168, 189, 190; purchase discount, see Purchase, discount; ratios, 168, 190, 191; real estate dealer, 25; report form, 24–26, 220, 221; results of operations for a specific period of time, 2, 3, 13, 22; sales discount, 26, 27, 29, 75, 181; sales section, 24–27; schedules, 33, 167–169, 191, 192, 213, 217, 220, 221; sections, 24–30; single-step, 24, 25; vertical form, 24
Income summary account, 38, 39, 62, 66–68, 115, 119, 133
Income taxes, 6, 20, 220
Independent auditor, 192
Index to accounts, 45, 46
Indirect labor, 164, 165
Individual proprietorship. See Single proprietorship
Industrial accounting, 161–171

Job order sheet, 163, 170
Journal, 50–55, 84–100; account
type, 86, 87; adjusting entry,
58–61, 67, 91; analysis of transactions, 51; and ledger, basic
books, 55; book of original, or
first, entry, 41, 48, 51, 55; cash,
86–88, 90, 100, 102, 129; cashbook, 88; cashbook and journal,
86; check register, 102, 110,
111; chronological record, 51,
55; closing entry, 61, 62, 67, 91;
columnar, 52, 84–90, 95–100;
combination, 86; combined
cash, 86; compound entry, 54,
91, 142, 144, 145; correcting
entry, 59, 91; defined, 51, 52;
departmentalized, 172, 173;
divided-column, 52, 84–90,
95–100; entry defined, 52;
entry described, 52–55, 66–68,
85–87, 95–100, 107, 135, 144,
145; finished goods record,
163; form, 52, 54, 85, 89; general, 52, 84–91; general ledger
column, 85; general, not supplanted, 85, 97; journalizing
groups of transactions, 52, 98;
journal-ledger, 86, 87; journal
voucher, 105; legal evidence,
55; multiple-column, 90; need
for subdivision, 84; notes payable register, 101, 102; notes
receivable register, 88, 101,
102; opening entry, 54, 91;
periodic entry, 58, 59; post-
closing entry, 63, 64, 91; posting, 54, 55, 89, 90, 97–100,
111; private, 88, 89; pro forma
entry, 126, 127, 144; proving,
97; purchase, 88, 102, 110, 173;
readjusting entry, 63, 64;
record, 88; register, 88, 101,
102, 110; relationship to ledger,
55; requisition, 88; reversal entry, 63, 64; reversing entry, 63,
64; sales, 88–90, 102, 187, 202;
sales returns and allowances, 88;
simple, 52; simple entry, 54;
single-column, 89, 90; special,
see Special journal; special-
column, 52, 84–90, 95–100;

standard form, 52–54; stock
transfer, 130; subscribers' cash
receipts, 129; sundry column,
85, 97–99, 110, 111; synoptic,
87; two-column, 52–55, 84–86;
voucher, 105; voucher register,
88, 102, 110, 111
Journal of Accountancy, 194
Journalizing, 52–55, 98

Labor, 73, 91, 95, 162–165
Land, 11, 15, 153, 217, 218
Large-scale production, 1, 161, 162,
176
Last-in, first-out, or lifo, inventory
pricing, 73
Law related to accounting, 8
Leaseholds, 11, 166
Ledger, 41–49, 91–100; accounts
payable, 92, 110, 111; accounts
receivable, 92; alone not satisfactory, 50; analytical record,
41, 55; and journal, basic
books, 55; auxiliary, 166; balanced periodically, 99; bound,
41; branch, 94, 95, 175; capital stock, 92, 123, 129, 130;
chronological history absent,
50; columnar account, 87, 94;
controlling accounts, see Controlling account; creditors', 92,
111; cumulative analysis, 50,
111; customers', 92; defined,
41, 50, 51; derived record, 41,
55; expense, 92; factory, 92,
94, 95, 166, 167; finished
goods, 163, 164; functions of
a columnar ledger account, 87;
general, 87, 89, 91–95, 98, 99,
166, 175; group of accounts, 41;
in balance, 46; in balance periodically, 99; incomplete record,
50, 51; index, 45, 46; job cost,
163; journal-ledger, 86, 87;
loose-leaf, 41; need for subdivision, 84; plant, 92, 166;
posting, 54, 55, 89, 90, 97–
100; private 89, 92; purchase,
92, relationship to journal, 55;
sales, 92, 187; secondary record,
41; self-balancing special, 94,
95, 166, 167, 175; special, see